THE CULT OF OTHIN

AN ESSAY IN
THE ANCIENT RELIGION OF
THE NORTH

BY

H. M. CHADWICK

FELLOW OF CLARE COLLEGE, CAMBRIDGE.

LONDON:

C. J. CLAY AND SONS,

CAMBRIDGE UNIVERSITY PRESS WAREHOUSE,

AVE MARIA LANE.

1899

CAMBRIDGE UNIVERSITY PRESS
Cambridge, New York, Melbourne, Madrid, Cape Town,
Singapore, São Paulo, Delhi, Mexico City

Cambridge University Press
The Edinburgh Building, Cambridge CB2 8RU, UK

Published in the United States of America by Cambridge University Press, New York

www.cambridge.org
Information on this title: www.cambridge.org/9781107677197

First published 1899
First paperback edition 2013

A catalogue record for this publication is available from the British Library

ISBN 978-1-107-67719-7 Paperback

CONTENTS.

			PAGE
INTRODUCTION		. . . .	1
CHAPTER I.	The cult of Othin in the North . . .	3
„ II.	Traces of the cult of Woden on the Continent and in Britain	29
„ III.	The introduction of the cult into the North	49
NOTE I.	The name of the god	66
„ II.	The story of Starkaðr	68
„ III.	The interpretation of Hávamál 138 f. . .	72

PREFACE.

THE following essay is an attempt to answer certain questions in regard to the character of one of the ancient Germanic cults. References to mythology have been as far as possible avoided except in Note III. In this case a reference to the Yggdrasill myth seemed to be necessitated by Bugge's *Studier over de nordiske Gude- og Heltesagns Oprindelse,* for the theory propounded by Bugge affects the whole character of the Northern cult. The myth is clearly connected with the rite of tree-hanging which formed an important though possibly not an original feature in the cult.

Some apology is perhaps needed for the extensive use which I have made of the collection of sagas published in Rafn's *Fornaldar Sögur.* While admitting the lateness of the sagas themselves, I believe that much of the material which they contain is considerably older. At all events the more important of the stories here quoted occur also in Saxo or other early authorities.

In conclusion I have to express my obligations to several friends for valuable information and for assistance kindly given to me in various ways.

H. M. CHADWICK.

CAMBRIDGE,
April, 1899.

ABBREVIATIONS.

O. E. = Old English.

O. H. G. = Old High German.

O. N. = Old Norse.

O. Sax. = Old Saxon.

s. = saga.

F. A. S. = Fornaldar Sögur.

Vǫl. R. = Vǫluspá, Codex Regius.

P. B. B. = Paul-Braunes Beiträge.

Z. f. d. A. = Zeitschrift für deutsches Alterthum.

INTRODUCTION.

FEW of the ancient Germanic cults exercised a more important influence on the character and fortunes of the race than that of Woden. Yet in spite of this fact, not only the origin but even the character of the cult is shrouded in much obscurity. This is due partly to the scantiness of the evidence in England and on the Continent, partly to the fact that in the North, where the materials are much more plentiful, it is by no means unlikely that cults of essentially different character became confused even before the end of heathen times. In one respect a fairly satisfactory conclusion seems to have been reached in recent years; Petersen's work "Om Nordboernes gudekyrkelse og gudetro i hedenold" (1876) has rendered it probable that the cult of Woden (Othin) was not native in the North. Another conclusion which has found general acceptance, namely, that the cult was never practised by the tribes of Upper Germany, seems to me less certain, as it is based entirely on negative evidence.

The myths connected with Othin have been frequently discussed, but sufficient attention has hardly been paid to the cult itself and the rites with which it was associated. In the following pages an attempt will be made to examine this subject with a view to obtaining answers to the following questions: 1. What were the characteristics

C.   1

of the cult in the North ? 2. Is this cult approximately identical with that of the ancient (continental) Germans, or has it undergone substantial modifications in the North ? 3. When was the cult introduced into the North ?

In regard to the origin of the cult, it seems to me that we are not yet in a position to arrive at any satisfactory conclusion. I am not convinced that " Woden is the deified Wode " and that the cult is an outgrowth of the belief known as " das wütende Heer." On the contrary I suspect that its origin is rather to be sought outside the Germanic area, probably either among the Gauls or among the races inhabiting the basin of the Danube. Another difficult question closely bound up with the preceding is the relationship between Woden-Othin and the Germanic " Mars " (O.H.G. *Zio*, O.E. *Tī*, *Tiw-*, O.N. *Týr*), a deity who, to judge from his name (originally *Tiwaz, " god "), must once have occupied a peculiar position in the Germanic theology. It is possible that the Northern Othin, perhaps even the Wōðenaz-Mercurius of the first century, may have had some of the attributes of this (probably older) deity transferred to him. Of the god Tīwaz however but little is known, though he has been the subject of much unprofitable speculation. For the present I prefer to avoid discussing this question.

CHAPTER I.

ALLUSIONS to sacrifices offered to Othin on the battle-field are frequent. These sacrifices however must be discussed together with other rites connected with the cult of Othin in time of war. Sacrifices under other circumstances are not unfrequently mentioned, but the god to whom the sacrifice was offered is not usually specified. In cases where it is distinctly stated that the sacrifice was offered to Othin, the victims are, so far as I am aware, always human. This however may be an accident as the number of examples is small. The most striking case is the sacrifice of king Vikar, which is recorded in Gautreks s. konungs c. 7 (F. A. S. III. p. 31 ff.) and Saxo VI. p. 276 f. According to the account given in Gautreks Saga, Vikar's fleet was delayed by contrary winds. Having had recourse to divination, they find that Othin requires a man out of their company. The victim is to be chosen by lot and hanged. Selection by lot is therefore made throughout the host, and the lot falls on the king. After this the Saga goes on to relate Starkaðr's vision in the forest (cf. p. 68 f.). At the conclusion of the discussion Hrosshársgrani (Othin) asks Starkaðr to reward him for the services which he has rendered him, and to this Starkaðr consents. Hrosshársgrani then says that he

The worship of Othin by sacrifice.

1—2

requires Vikar to be sent to him and instructs Starkaðr how this is to be done. He gives Starkaðr a javelin and tells him that this will appear to be a reed-cane. After this they return to the host, and the following morning the king's councillors meet to consider what is to be done. They all agree that the sacrifice should be carried out in form only, to which end Starkaðr proposes a plan. In the neighbourhood was a fir tree and close by it a tall stump, over which a long thin branch hung down from the upper part of the tree. The servants were at the time preparing a meal, and had killed and cut up a calf. Starkaðr took some of the calf's entrails and, climbing on to the stump, pulled down the branch and tied the strings on to it. Then he said to the king, " Here is a gallows ready for you, O king, and I do not think it looks very dangerous." The king climbed on to the stump, and Starkaðr laid the noose round his neck and leaped down. Then he thrust against the king with his cane saying, "Now I give thee to Othin," and released the branch. The cane turned into a javelin and transfixed the king, the stump fell from beneath his feet, and the strings turned into strong withies; the branch flew back and swept the king into the tree-top, and there he died.

According to Ynglinga s. 29, Aun, king of Sweden, sacrificed to Othin for length of life, and obtained the answer that he should live so long as he sacrificed one of his sons every tenth year. In this way nine of his ten sons were sacrificed. Again, according to Ynglinga s. 47, there was a famine in the reign of Ólafr Trételgi, which the people attributed to the fact that Ólafr was not zealous in sacrificing. They therefore "burnt him in his house and gave him to Othin, sacrificing him that they themselves might have plenty[1]." With this passage may

[1] brendu hann inni ok gáfu hann Óðni ok blétu honum til árs sér.

be compared Hervarar s. ok Heiðreks konungs, c. 11, 12 (F. A. S. I. 451 ff.), which describes how a famine arose in Reiðgotaland during the reign of king Haraldr. It was found by divination that the famine could only be stopped by the sacrifice of the noblest youth in the land. It was unanimously agreed that Angantýr, son of Heiðrekr, was the person required. Heiðrekr however took counsel to avoid this, and determined to offer the king with his son Halfdan and all their host as a sacrifice to Othin in place of his own son. He therefore attacked and slew them, and "had the temples reddened with the blood of Haraldr and Halfdan, and committed to Othin all the host that had fallen, as an offering for plenty in place of his son."

Besides these occasional sacrifices it is probable that sacrifices to Othin were offered also at certain fixed festivals. The heathen Scandinavians had three great annual sacrifices, which are thus described in Ynglinga s. 8: (1) *í móti vetri til árs*, "at the approach of winter; (this sacrifice was) for plenty": (2) *at miðium vetri til gróðrar*, "at midwinter for increase (of the crops)": (3) *at sumri, þat var sigrblót*, "at the beginning of summer; this was a sacrifice for victory." The first of these sacrifices was certainly connected with the worship of Frö; the second probably with that of Thor[1]. It is probable also that the third of these sacrifices (the sacrifice for victory) was associated with Othin. This is shown by the constant references to Othin as the giver of victory; by his name *Sigtýr*, "god of victory"; by sacrifices and vows made to Othin for victory in time of war, examples of which will be given in the following pages; lastly by the custom observed in the drinking of toasts, which is thus described in Hákonar s. góða, c. 16:

[1] Cf. Adam of Bremen IV. 26. Thor...uentos ymbresque serena et fruges gubernat.

"It was customary first to drink Othin's toast for victory and for the glory of their king, and after that the toasts of Niǫrðr and Frö for plenty and peace." Besides these annual festivals there were sacrifices on a great scale every nine years at Upsala and Leire[1], at which sacrifices of men together with various animals were offered. According to Schol. 137 to Adam of Bremen the sacrifice at Upsala took place about the spring equinox; it would coincide therefore with the annual sacrifice for victory. Consequently it is not unlikely that this sacrifice also was connected with the worship of Othin. At Leire indeed the corresponding sacrifice took place in January. It is possible however that the arrangement of the annual sacrifices in Denmark was not the same as in Norway and Sweden.

According to Adam of Bremen IV. 27 sacrifice was offered by the Swedes to Othin on the ap-proach of war[2]. It seems to have been at one time a common practice to sacrifice notable prisoners taken in war. In the account of the battle in Egils s. ok Ásmundar c. 8 (F. A. S. III. p. 379) it is stated that "all Ásmundr's men had fallen and he was himself taken prisoner; it was then evening; they had decided to slay him on the morrow at Aran's tomb, and give him to Othin that they might themselves have victory" (*gefa hann Óðni til sigrs sér*). The same phrase is used in Orkn. saga c. 8, where it is related that Ragnar's sons captured Ella and put him to death by cutting the "blood-eagle" upon his back (cf. Ragnars s. Loðbrókar, c. 18; Saxo IX. p. 463). It is probable also that the hanging of captured enemies was regarded as a sacrifice to Othin. This custom is frequently mentioned, especially

The cult of Othin in time of war.

[1] Cf. Adam of Bremen, IV. 27; Thietmar, Chron. I. 9.
[2] Si pestis et famis imminet Thor ydolo libatur, si bellum Wodani.

in stories which deal with the reign of Iǫrmunrekr (cf. p. 17).

The dedication of an enemy's army to Othin before the commencement of a battle must also have been regarded as a sacrificial act. According to Eyrbyggia s. 44 it was the custom in ancient times to shoot a javelin over the enemy's army, in order to turn the luck in one's own favour[1]. That this custom was connected with the cult of Othin is shown by the following examples: In Hervarar s. ok Heiðreks c. 18 (F. A. S. I. 501), before the battle between the Reiðgotar and the Huns, Gizr rode up to the Huns' army and said: "Your king is panic-stricken, your leader is doomed,...Othin is wroth with you;...may Othin let the dart fly according to my words." So also in Styrbiarnar þáttr c. 2: Before his battle with Styrbiǫrn Eirekr went into Othin's temple and devoted himself to die after ten years, if he might obtain the victory; shortly afterwards he saw a tall man with a long hood, who gave him a cane and told him to shoot it over Styrbiǫrn's army with these words: "Ye all belong to Othin[2]." This example is remarkable because the battle is a historical event and seems to have taken place about 960—970 (cf. Saxo x. p. 479). According to the Saga af Haraldi Gráfeld c. 11, Eirekr died ten years after Styrbiǫrn's fall. With the phrase "Ye all belong to Othin" may be compared Saxo VII. p. 361, where it is stated that Haraldus (i.e. Haraldr Hilditǫnn, king of Denmark) had acquired the favour of Othin to such an extent that the latter granted him immunity from wounds in war. In return for this Haraldus "is said to have promised to Othin the souls which he ejected from their bodies by the sword."

[1] þá skaut Steinþórr spióti at fornum sið til heilla sér yfir flokk Snorra.

[2] Óðinn á yðr alla.

According to Saxo VIII. p. 390 Haraldus repeated this vow in his last fight, in order that he might obtain the victory against Ringo (i.e. Sigurðr Hringr). In the Sǫgubrot af Fornkonungum, c. 8 (F. A. S. I. 380) the words of this vow are given as follows: "I give to Othin (*gef ek Óðni*) all the host which falls in this battle." It is noticeable that this is the sacrificial formula (cf. p. 4). Again, according to Saxo IX. p. 446, Syuardus (i.e. Sigurðr orm í auga, son of Ragnar Loðbrók) was so severely wounded that the physicians despaired of his life, when a certain man of immense size approached his couch and promised to restore him to health forthwith "if he would devote to him the souls of those whom he should destroy in war[1]." He declared that his name was Rostarus.

But further, the slaying of an enemy in battle under ordinary circumstances seems to have been regarded as a sacrifice to Othin. This is shown by a verse in Skaldskaparmal, c. 1, attributed to Thióðolfr: "There lay the dead on the sand, allotted to Frigg's one-eyed husband; we rejoiced at such a deed[2]." With this may be compared Islendinga s. I. p. 307, where Helgi after killing Thorgrimr in battle sings: "I have given the brave son of Thormóðr to Othin; we have offered him as a sacrifice to the ruler of the gallows, and his corpse to the raven[3]." In this passage the phrase "give to Othin" is practically equivalent to "slay in battle." In like manner the phrases "go to Othin" and "receive Othin's hospitality" are used as equivalent to "be slain in battle," e.g. in Ragnars s. Loðbrókar, c. 9 (F. A. S. I. 265), when Aslaug hears of

---

[1] Si sibi illorum quos armis oppressurus foret animas dedicasset.

[2] valr lá þar á sandi vitinn inum eineygia
Friggiar faðmbyggvi. fǫgnuðum dáð slíkri.

[3] Ásmóðar gaf ek Óðni arfa þróttar diarfan,
guldum galgavaldi Gautstafn en ná hrafni.

her son's death, she says :—" Rǫgnvaldr began to stain his
shield with the blood of men; he, the youngest of my
sons, in his terrible valour has come to Othin[1]."

In Hrómundar s. Greipssonar, c. 2 (F. A. S. II. 366),
Kari, when mortally wounded, says to the king :—" Fare-
well, I am going to be Othin's guest[2]." So also in the
account of the fight between Hialmar and Oddr and the
twelve "berserkir" in Hervarar s. ok Heiðreks, c. 5
(F. A. S. I. 422 f.), Hialmar says to Oddr: "It seems to
me very likely that we shall all be Othin's guests in
Valhǫll to-night[3]." Oddr answers: "It is not I who shall
be Othin's guest to-night, but they will all be dead before
night comes, and we shall be alive." In the verse the
dialogue runs thus : H. "We two brave warriors shall be
Othin's guests this evening, but those twelve will live."
O. "They will be Othin's guests this evening, the twelve
berserkir, but we two shall live[4]." The synonymous
phrase í Valhǫll gista ('lodge in Valhǫll') occurs in
Hrólfs s. Kraka 51 (F. A. S. I. 106).

It has already been pointed out that the phrase "give
to Othin" is applied both to sacrifice and to the slaying
of an enemy. By itself the meaning of this phrase might
be ambiguous; the expression "become Othin's guest"
however can have only one meaning, namely that the
person of whom it was used must have been regarded
as still existing after death in some close relationship
to Othin. That persons killed in battle were regarded
as passing into Othin's presence is shown by the names

[1] Rǫgnvaldr tók at rióða rǫnd í gumna blóði;
  hann kom yngstr til Óðins ógndiarfr sona mínna.

[2] ek man hiá Óðni gista.

[3] at vér munum allir Óðinn gista í Valhǫll í kvǫld.

[4] H. við munum í aptan Óðinn gista
     tveir fullhugar, en þeir tolf lifa.
   O. ...þeir munu í aptan Óðinn gista
     tolf berserkir, en við tveir lifa.

Val-fǫðr, "father of the slain," applied to Othin himself,
and *Val-hǫll*, "hall of the slain," applied to Othin's
dwelling; so also by such passages as the following:—
"The fifth dwelling is called 'Glaðsheimr,' where Valhǫll
bright with gold stands wide outspread; there Hroptr
(i.e. Othin) chooses every day men who die by arms."
Grímnismál, v. 8[1]. So also Krakumál, v. 29 (F. A. S. I.
310):—..."The Disir (i.e. Valkyries) summon me home;
Othin has sent them to me from Herjan's hall; I will
gladly drink ale in the highseat among the Aesir...[2]."
Ragnar Loðbrók, however, whose last words are here
given, did not die actually in battle but was put to death
afterwards by means of poisonous snakes. In Helgakviða
Hundingsbana, II. 37 f., the slain Helgi is represented as
coming to Valhǫll and there meeting his old enemy
Hundingr. Othin offers Helgi a share in all his power.
The entrance of a slain man into Valhǫll forms the
subject also of the poems Eireksmál and Hákonarmál.
In the latter poem the Val-kyriur, "choosers of the slain,"
figure prominently. But it is at least questionable if in
actual religious belief they occupied the same position
which is ascribed to them in the poetry. They are
elsewhere (Vǫlsunga s. 2 etc.) called Othin's *óskmeyiar*
"adopted maidens" (or "daughters"). With this may be
compared the expression *óskasynir*, "adopted sons," in
Gylf. 20: "all those who fall in battle are called Othin's

[1] Glaðsheimr heitir inn fimti,
þars in gullbiarta
Valhǫll víð of þrumir;
en þar Hroptr
kýss hverian dag
vápndauða vera.

[2] ...heim bióða mér Dísir,
sem frá Herians hǫllu
hefir Óðinn mér sendar;
glaðr skal ek ǫl með Asum
í ǫndvegi drekka.......

óskasynir." The more usual term for the latter is however *einheriar*, which signifies perhaps merely "champions." Their life is described in Vafþrúðnismál 41 (cf. Grímn. 23).

The belief in immortality in connection with the cult of Othin is stated as follows in Ynglinga s. 10:—"The Swedes often thought that Othin appeared to them when a great battle was impending; to some he gave victory, while others he summoned to him; either alternative seemed good[1]." This attitude of mind was displayed by Sigmundr, who, when he lay mortally wounded, spoke as follows (Vǫlsunga s. 12):—"It is Othin's will that we shall no longer draw the sword, now that it is broken; I have fought so long as it pleased him;......I will now go to seek our kinsfolk who are already departed." This is to be compared with Ynglinga s. 10, where Othin on his deathbed is represented as saying that he was about to go to Goðheimr and to greet his friends there. It is likely however that these passages are due to the influence of Christian ideas. The heathen spirit is more clearly to be discerned in the dying words of Ragnar Loðbrók (Kraku-mál 29, cf. p. 10): "I will gladly drink ale on the highseat among the Aesir; the hours of my life are ended; I will die laughing[2]." But the view that "either alternative (victory or death) was good" did not always prevail. Thus in Halfs s. 13 (F. A. S. II. 45), when King Halfr has fallen with a great part of his army, Innsteinn, one of his followers, says:—"We owe Othin an evil reward for robbing such a king of victory[3]." So also in Saga

---

[1] gaf hann þá sumum sigr, en sumum bauð hann til sín; þótti hvárr-tveggi kostr góðr.

[2] ...lífs eru liðnar stundir
læiandi skal ek deyia.

[3] egum Óðni illt at gialda
er hann slíkan konung sigri rænti.

Ketils hængs 5 (F. A. S. II. 132 ff., 139), Framarr, to whom
Othin had granted victory and immunity from the effects
of iron, says, when mortally wounded :—" Balder's father
has now broken faith; it is unsafe to trust him[1]." Othin
is represented as turning against his heroes at the last.
Another example occurs in Saxo's account of the 'bellum
Brauicum' (VIII. p. 390), where Haraldus finds that Othin
has betrayed the secret of the 'wedge' (see p. 21) to his
rival Ringo.   He then discovers that Othin has taken the
place of his councillor Bruno and is acting as charioteer
to him.   In spite of his prayers, Bruno throws Haraldus
down to the ground and kills him.   So also in Saxo v. p.
238) the army of the Huns in its distress is deserted by a
certain 'Uggerus uates' of uncertain though more than
human age.   This man, who is clearly Othin (Icel. *Yggr*),
goes over to Frotho and betrays to him the plans of the
Huns.   Othin is called "faithless" also in Hrólfs s. Kraka
c. 51 (F. A. S. I. 107), where Boðvar Biarki looking on the
ranks of the enemy says that he can not discern Othin, yet
strongly suspects that he is flitting about amongst them,
" the foul and faithless son of Herian."   Othin's unfairness is made a taunt against him in Lokasenna 22;
Loki says :—" Be silent, Othin, thou hast never been able
to order the course of war (fairly); often hast thou given
victory to cowards, who did not deserve it[2]" (cf. also
Hárbarðslióð 25).   An explanation of Othin's inconstancy
and unfairness is suggested in Eireksmál 24 ff.; when
Othin praises Eirekr, who is now approaching the gate of
Valhǫll, Sigmundr asks him: "Why hast thou deprived

---

[1] brást nú Baldurs faðir ; brigt er at trúa honum.

[2] þegi þú, Óðinn, þú kunnir aldrigi
   deila víg meÞ verum ;
   opt þu gaft þeim er þú gefa skyldira,
   enum slævurum, sigr.

him of victory if thou thoughtest him to be brave?"
Othin answers: "Because it cannot clearly be known when
the gray wolf shall come against the abodes of the gods[1]."
The meaning obviously is that Othin wishes to have great
champions amongst his 'Einheriar' to help him in his
struggle against the wolf. So also in Grímnismál 23 the
Einheriar are represented as going forth to battle against
the hostile powers.

It is still doubtful how great an antiquity can be
claimed for the Scandinavian doctrine concerning the end
of the world. Until this is settled it is clearly impossible
to decide whether the explanation of Othin's inconstancy
given in Eireksmál is in accordance with ancient belief or
is a conception of the tenth century poets. It has been
shown in the preceding pages that persons killed in battle
were regarded as passing to Valhǫll. Now since Othin's
heroes usually fell in battle, and Othin had the control
over victory and death (cf. p. 11), it follows that, as soon
as death in battle came to be regarded as undesirable, a
belief in Othin's inconstancy must necessarily arise, and
some explanation of this inconstancy be furnished[2].

There seem to be traces of one other sacrificial or
semi-sacrificial rite connected with the cult of Othin. In
the Ynglinga saga Othin is represented as a king who had
once ruled in Sweden. The account of his life ends as
follows (c. 10):—" Othin died of sickness in Sweden; and
when he was at death's door he had himself marked with

[1] S. hví namtu hann sigri þá ef þér þótti hann sniallr vesa?
O. því at óvist es at vita
nær úlfr inn hǫsvi
gengr á siǫt goða.

[2] It is difficult to reconcile this explanation with the existence of the
belief in metempsychosis. That a belief of this kind prevailed, to some
extent at least, is shown especially by the prose passage at the end of
Helgakviþa Hundingsbana II.

the point of a javelin and appropriated to himself all
men who met their death by arms; he said that he was
about to go to Goðheimr and greet his friends there[1]."
That this is to be regarded as the establishment of a
custom is made probable by the description of the death
of Niǫrðr in the following chapter:—"Niǫrðr died of
sickness; he also had himself marked for Othin before he
died[2]." There are no certain references to such a custom
elsewhere, so far as I am aware. But in Hyndlulióð 28,
after the enumeration of Óttarr's ancestors, the following
sentence occurs (referring perhaps only to the persons
mentioned in the same verse): "They were men marked
with a sign for the gods[3]." It is remarkable that the same
expression is used by Starkaðr in Gautreks s. 7 (F. S. A.
III. 35), when he is describing the sacrifice of Vikar: "I
had to mark (or possibly "decided to mark") Vikar with
a sign for the gods[4]." If this refers to his stabbing Vikar
with Othin's javelin (cf. p. 4), the passage in Hyndlulióð
may very well be a reminiscence of some such rite as that
described in Ynglinga s. 10, 11. At the same time,
however, the absence of evidence from any other source
must be taken as showing that the rite was not well
known, and probably not practised in the last days of
heathendom. The rite was clearly regarded by the writer
of Ynglinga saga as a substitution for death in battle.

In the account of the sacrifice of Vikar in Gautreks
s. 7 (see p. 3 f.) the complicated nature of the
ceremonial, above all the combination of stabbing and hanging at the same time, would naturally lead

The ritual
of sacrifice.

[1] Óðinn varð sóttdauðr í Svíþióð; ok er hann var at kominn bana,
lét hann marka sik geirsoddi ok eignaði sér alla vápndauða menn etc.

[2] Niǫrðr varð sóttdauðr, lét hann ok marka sik Óðni áðr hann dó.

[3] þeir váru gumnar goðum signaðir.

[4] skylda (skilda MSS.) ek Vikar...goðum um signa.

one to the conclusion that the story gives a more or less faithful picture of the ritual actually employed in sacrifice to Othin. It is true that the present text of the saga is late, but since the story was known to Saxo (VI. p. 276 f.) in practically the same form, it must have been current at any rate before the end of the 12th century, that is to say not more than 100—150 years after human sacrifices had ceased to be practised. Bugge however (Studier over de nordiske Gude- og Heltesagns Oprindelse, p. 315) holds that the story has been affected by a myth to which reference is made in Hávamál 138 :—"I know that I hung full nine nights on the gallows (or 'windy tree') wounded by the javelin and given to Othin, myself to myself" etc[1]. It seems to me totally unnecessary to suppose that the account of the Vikar-sacrifice has been built up out of this myth. But, as the question has been raised, it will be well to examine other passages in which sacrifices are described, with a view to ascertaining, if possible, the means employed for putting the victim to death.

Apart from the two examples mentioned above there is no example of the employment of hanging and stabbing combined[2]. Indeed, apart from these cases, there is no example of the stabbing of a victim[3]. Yet the javelin is frequently associated with Othin. His own peculiar weapon is the javelin Gungnir (Skaldsk. 3). It is with a javelin

[1] veit ek at ek hekk
vindga meiði á
nætr allar níu,
geiri undaðr
ok gefinn Óðni,
siálfr siálfum mér etc.

[2] Cf. however the story of Ibn Fazlan, p. 43.

[3] The javelin is used for killing Eirekr son of Ragnar Loðbrók in Ragnars s. L. 9 (F.A.S. I. 262 f.). It is not distinctly stated that this was a sacrifice, but it can hardly have been otherwise.

that he has himself marked before his death according to
Yngl. 10 (cf. p. 13 f.). When Dagr sacrifices to Othin
(Helgakv. Hundingsbana II. 27, prose), Othin lends him
his javelin, with which he stabs Helgi. So also in Vol-
sunga s. 11 (F.A.S. I. 145) Sigmundr in his last battle
met a man who had one eye and held a javelin in his
hand. When Sigmundr attacked him with his sword he
received the blow on his javelin; the sword then snapped
in two pieces. So again in Egils s. ok Ásmundar c. 17
(F.A.S. III. 407) Othin is said to have stabbed Ásmundr
with his javelin. The practice of dedicating the enemy to
Othin by throwing a javelin over their army (cf. p. 7)
may also be compared.

References to sacrificial hanging are fairly frequent.
At the great festival which, according to Adam of Bremen,
(IV. 27) took place every nine years at Upsala (cf. p. 6),
the bodies of the victims, human and animal alike, were
hung in the grove close to the temple[1]. It has been
shown (p. 6) that it was customary to put to death
prisoners captured in war as a sacrifice to Othin. Such
persons appear to have been frequently hanged. Thus
according to Ynglinga s. 26 Iǫrundr and Eirikr captured
Guðlaugr, king of the Háleygir, and hanged him. In
Yngl. 28 Gýlaugr son of Guðlaugr captures and hangs
Iǫrundr. In the verse quoted from Thióðolfr in this passage
the gallows is called "Sleipnir"—the name of Othin's
horse[2]. So also with persons arrested in acts of hostility
or trespass generally. Thus in Saxo I. p. 28 Gro warns
Bessus that her father Sigtrug will overcome and hang
him. Several cases of hanging occur in the cycle of

[1] Corpora autem suspenduntur in lucum qui proximus est templo.

[2] The hanging of prisoners captured in war seems to have been
practised occasionally even down to historical times, e.g. Olafs s.
Tryggvasonar (Heimskringla) c. 14, where Hákon hangs Gullharaldr.

stories relating to Iǫrmunrekr[1]. Thus according to Saxo
VIII. p. 411 Iarmericus captured and hanged forty Slavs,
hanging wolves with them. Saxo adds that this insulting
punishment was formerly reserved for persons who had
been guilty of "parricidium." According to Saxo VIII. p. 413
Iarmericus hanged his nephews, whom he had captured
in war. In Hamðismál 18 Hamðir and Sǫrli, on their
arrival at the court of Iǫrmunrekr, find "their" (or "his")
"sister's son hanging wounded on the beam, the wind-cold
tree of the criminal, west of the palace." Possibly this
is a reference to the same event. In v. 22 of the same
poem Iǫrmunrekr commands his men to hang Hamðir
and Sǫrli. Hanging was a frequent method of executing
capital punishment, especially, it seems, in the case of
persons guilty of adultery or seduction. The most famous
case is the hanging of Hagbarðr (Hagbarthus; Saxo VII.
p. 345), to which reference is frequently made in Scandinavian poetry. So also, according to Skáldskaparmál 47,
Iǫrmunrekr has his son Randver hanged, when he hears
that he has committed adultery with his wife Svanhildr.
In Saxo's account (VIII. p. 413 f.) of the same event, where
Randver is called Broderus, the punishment is only formal.
A case of suicide by hanging is given by Saxo I. p. 60.
Hundingus had been drowned in a vat at a wake held
through false news of Hadingus' death; Hadingus on
hearing the news hanged himself in the sight of his people.
There are two examples from foreign sources which prove
the great antiquity of sacrificial hanging among the Swedes.
Procopius (Gothic War II. 15) says that the sacrifice which
is most valued by the people of Thule (i.e. Sweden and
Norway), is that of the first man whom they capture in
war. "This sacrifice they offer to Ares since they believe

[1] If the legends are true, these can not of course be accepted as
evidence for a Scandinavian custom.

him to be the greatest of the gods. They sacrifice the
prisoner not merely by slaughtering him but by hanging
him from a beam, or casting him among thorns, or putting
him to death by other horrible methods[1]." In Beowulf 2939
the Swedish king Ongenþeo, after slaying Hæðcyn, king
of the Geatas, and besieging the remnants of his army in a
wood, is represented as threatening the fugitives "that in
the morning he would destroy them with the edge of the
sword; some he would hang on gallows-trees as a joy to
the birds (?)[2]." The period, to which Procopius' information about "Thule" applies, is the first half of the sixth
century. In all probability the same is true also of
Beowulf (cf. p. 50), though Ongenþeo, who is rather a
person of the past to the chief characters in the story,
may have died before A.D. 500.

It is true that Othin is not mentioned in any of these
passages, except in the one quoted from Procopius, where
Ares is probably meant for Othin[3]. Yet that these sacri-

---

[1] τῶν δὲ ἱερείων σφίσι τὸ κάλλιστον ἄνθρωπός ἐστιν ὅνπερ ἂν δοριάλωτον
ποιήσαιντο πρῶτον. τοῦτον γὰρ τῷ Ἄρει θύουσιν ἐπεὶ θεὸν αὐτὸν νομίζουσι
μέγιστον εἶναι. ἱερῶνται δὲ καὶ τὸν αἰχμάλωτον οὐ θύοντες μόνον ἀλλὰ καὶ
ἀπὸ ξύλου κρεμῶντες ἢ ἐς τὰς ἀκάνθας ῥιπτοῦντες ταῖς ἄλλαις τε κτείναντες
θανάτου ἰδέαις οἰκτίσταις.

[2]   cwæð he on mergenne meces ecgum
     getan wolde, sum(e) on galgtreowu(m)
     (fuglum) to gamene.
the bracketed letters have been added as the text is defective.

[3] For the identification of Othin with Mars the following passages
may be compared:—

Saxo II. p. 106.   Biarco : Et nunc ille ubi sit qui uulgo dicitur Othin etc.
           Ruta :   Adde oculum propius et nostras prospice chelas,
                 ante sacraturus uictrici lumina signo,
                 si uis presentem tuto cognoscere Martem.
Saxo VIII. p. 399.   Castra quietis inops colui, pacemque perosus
                 sub signis, Gradiue, tuis discrimine summo
                 consenui.
That Gradiuus is here meant for Othin is shown by the fact that
Starcatherus, in whose mouth these words are put, was Othin's foster-son.

fices were intended for him is made probable by the
following considerations : (1) It was customary to sacrifice
prisoners to Othin on the battlefield (cf. p. 6 ff.); there is
no record of such sacrifices being offered to any other god.
(2) There is no mention of hanging in sacrifices to other
gods. Human victims were indeed offered to Thor, but
these appear to have been put to death by being felled
with a club or other wooden instrument. On the other
hand the association of Othin with the gallows is frequently
mentioned. Among his names (besides *Galga-farmr*
"burden of the gallows," which perhaps has reference to
Háv. 138 f.), we find *Galga-gramr, Galga-valdr, Hanga-
dróttinn, Hanga-týr, Hanga-guð* etc., all denoting "lord" or
"god of the gallows." According to Ynglinga s. 7 Othin
was in the habit of sitting under a gallows. The passage
perhaps refers to an obscure verse of Hávamál (155), the
meaning of which seems to be as follows: "If I see a
strangled corpse swinging upon a tree, I cut and paint
'runes' (on the body ?) in such a way, that the man
comes and talks with me[1]." With this may be compared
an unpublished passage of Jómsvíkinga-drápa 3 quoted by
Vigfusson (Dict. p. 238 b): "I did not get the share of
Othin under the gallows"[2] which Vigfusson takes to mean
"I am no adept in poetry." There can be no reasonable
doubt that the hanging of prisoners taken in war was
regarded as a sacrifice to Othin. It is at least probable

Cf. Adam of Bremen IV. 26: Wodanem uero sculpunt armatum sicut
nostri Martem solent.

[1] ef ek sé á tré uppi
    váfa virgilná,
    svá ek ríst
    ok í runum fák
    at sá gengr gumi
    ok mælir við mik.

[2] nam ek eigi Yggiar feng und hanga.

also that in such cases as those quoted above, the hanging
of criminals was regarded in the same light. For the
close connection between sacrifice and capital punishment
it will be sufficient here to refer to Golther, Mythologie
p. 548 f.

Since therefore both the javelin and the gallows
appear to have been in a certain sense sacred to Othin,
and further since the javelin was used in dedicating
enemies and the gallows in sacrificing prisoners, it seems
to me unnecessary to suppose with Bugge that the story
of Vikar has been influenced by the myth related in
Háv. 138. On the contrary there is every probability
that it represents the ordinary ceremony of sacrifice; the
combination of hanging and stabbing being parallel to
the combination of strangling and stabbing in Ibn
Fazlan's story (p. 43). This was of course not the only
method of sacrificing to Othin. Another and simpler
plan was to set the house on fire when the victim was
asleep within (cf. Yngl. 47). The cutting of the 'blood-
eagle' upon Ella (Orkneyinga s. 8, Ragnars s. Loðbrókar
18, Saxo IX. p. 463; see p. 6) was a sacrifice; but there
is nothing to show that it was a rite of frequent
occurrence[1]. From the evidence which is at present
available there is every reason to suppose that hanging,
whether accompanied by stabbing or not, was the method
usually employed.

In Ynglinga s. 6 f. Othin is celebrated as the inventor
of poetry (skáldskapr), and as proficient in, if
not actually the inventor of incantations
(galdrar) and runes. To Othin also is
attributed (Yngl. 8) the establishment of the
three annual Swedish sacrifices. Besides
these, there are two institutions attributed to Othin

*Customs,
the institu-
tion of
which is
ascribed to
Othin.*

[1] Another case is mentioned in Reginsmál 26.

which require notice: (1) the 'wedge' order of battle, (2) Othin's ordinances in regard to the disposal of the dead.

1. The 'wedge' (O. Norse *rani, svínfylking, hamalt fylkia*) is known to Othin only, though it is taught by him to his heroes: e.g. in Sǫgubrot af fornkonungum 8 (F.A.S. I. 380). Haraldr (Hilditǫnn) says: "Who can have taught Hringr to draw up his army in wedge-shaped array (*hamalt at fylkia*); I thought this was known to none except myself and Othin. Does Othin wish to play me false in the awarding of victory?" In Saxo's account of the same event (VIII. p. 390) Haraldus is represented as asking whence Ringo could have derived this knowledge, "especially since Othynus was the teacher and inventor of this science, and no one except himself had received this new teaching in warfare." Othinus is represented as drawing up Haraldus' forces in this manner in his war against Ingo king of the Swedes (Saxo VII.. p. 363). So also in Saxo I. p. 52 f., when Hadingus is fighting against the Byarmenses, his army is drawn up in wedge-array by 'an old man' who is clearly Othin.

In connection with Othin's institutions in war a passage from Ynglinga s. 6 deserves mention: "Othin's men went without coats of mail and were raving like hounds or wolves; they bit into their shields and were as strong as bears or buffaloes; they slaughtered the enemy, and neither fire nor iron had any effect on them. This is called *berserksgangr*." Taken in connection with the fact that the javelin appears to be Othin's sacred weapon, this would seem to show that the worshippers of Othin at one time practised light-armed warfare, working themselves up into a frenzy before the battle began[1]. The

[1] The conception of the berserkr seems also to contain mythological features.

sword, helmet and mail coat are of course not unknown
to Othin, but they figure much less prominently than
the javelin.

2. Othin's funeral institutions are described in
Ynglinga s. 8 :—" He ordained that all dead men should
be burnt and brought on to the pyre with their property. He said that every dead man should come to
Valhǫll with such property as he had on the pyre; he
should also have the enjoyment of what he had himself buried in the earth. But the ashes were to be
carried out to sea or buried down in the earth. A
howe (mound) was to be raised as a memorial to
noblemen; and for all such persons as had achieved
any distinction 'bauta-stones' should be set up. This
custom lasted long after." As regards the nature of the
'property' thrown on to the pyre, it seems to have com-
prised not only arms, gold, silver and other such things,
but also animals, and occasionally even servants. Saxo
(VIII. p. 391) describes at length the burning of Haraldus
(Hilditǫnn). Ringo took his horse and harnessed it to
the royal chariot which was furnished with golden seats.
He laid the body of Haraldus in the chariot and prayed
that thus provided he might "arrive in Tartarus before
his comrades and beg Pluto, the lord of Orcus, to grant
peaceful abodes both for his allies and foes." He then
placed the chariot on the pyre, and, as the flames rose, he
implored his nobles to throw their arms, their gold, and
whatever wealth they had with them, unstintingly on to
the pyre, in honour of so great a king. In Sǫgubrot af
fornkonungum 9 (F.A.S. I. 387) the body of Haraldr is
buried in a howe, but otherwise the description of the
event agrees closely with that given by Saxo. " Hringr
had a great howe made, and had the body of Haraldr laid
in the chariot and driven therein to the howe with the

horse which Haraldr had had in the battle. The horse was then killed. Then King Hringr took the saddle on which he had himself ridden, and gave it to his kinsman, King Haraldr, and begged him to do whichever he wished, whether to ride or drive to Valhǫll. Then he had a great feast made in honour of the departure of his kinsman, King Haraldr. And before the howe was closed, King Hringr asked all his great men and all his champions who were present to cast great jewels and good weapons into the howe, in honour of King Haraldr Hilditǫnn: and afterwards the howe was carefully closed." So also at the burning of Balder described in Gylf. 49, Balder's horse and the ring Draupnir were laid on the pyre. At the funeral of Sigurðr and Brynhildr, described in Vǫlsunga s. 31 (F.A.S. I. 204), two hawks and a number of men-servants and maidservants were burnt[1]. In Ibn Fazlan's account of a 'Russian' funeral on the Volga there were burnt a young woman, a dog, a cock and hen, two horses and two oxen (cf. p. 43).

There is a most remarkable correspondence between the funeral rites described in the last section and the rites of sacrifice. It was believed that the spirits of the dead passed to Valhǫll, and it was for their use there that animals and other articles were burnt upon the pyre (cf. Yngl. s. 8). Perhaps the most striking illustration of this belief is the passage from Sǫgubrot af fornkonungum (c. 9), relating to the burial of Haraldr Hilditǫnn. Hringr gives Haraldr, together with a horse, both a chariot and a saddle, in order that he may have his choice of riding or driving to Valhǫll. But it has been shown above (p. 9 f.) that persons who were killed in battle were regarded as passing to Valhǫll, and

Conclusion : the character of the cult.

[1] Cf. Sigurðarkviða in skamma 67 ff., where modern editors have added 'two dogs.'

at the same time their death was regarded as a sacrifice
to Othin.   Even in other sacrifices the regular formula
employed, when slaying the victim, was 'I give thee to
Othin.'   The victim must therefore have been regarded
as passing to Valhǫll. This is confirmed by the expression
used in Gautreks s. 7, 'Othin desired a man out of their
company.'   The story of the sacrifice in Hervarar s. 11 f.
(cf. p. 5) affords a close parallel. The same idea also
underlies the story of Aun sacrificing his sons in Ynglinga
s. 29.   If further confirmation were needed it is supplied
by the following curious fact: at sacrifices—at all events
at the great nine-yearly sacrifices—animals were offered
together with men; these were, in part, not edible animals
such as were offered as a meal to Frö and other gods, but
precisely the same animals which were most usually burnt
upon the pyre at funerals, namely horses, dogs and hawks[1].
But, further, these animals seem to have been intended
rather for the use of the persons sacrificed, when they
arrived in Valhǫll, than as an offering to the gods.   This
is clearly shown by Thietmar's description of the sacrifice
at Leire (Thietmari Chronicon I. 9, M.G. III. p. 739):
" There is a general gathering at this place every nine
years, in the month of January, after the season at which
we celebrate the Epiphany.   Here they sacrifice to their
gods ninety-nine men and the same number of horses
together with dogs and cocks which they offer in place of
hawks.   They are convinced, as I have said, that these
animals will be at the service of the human victims when
they reach the powers below, and that they will appease
these powers for the sins which the men have committed[2]."

---

[1] Horses were certainly eaten by the ancient Scandinavians, but it is
not likely that dogs and hawks were ever used as articles of food in the
North.

[2] Est unus in his partibus locus...Lederun nomine...ubi post nouem

At the corresponding sacrifice at Upsala, described by Adam of Bremen (IV. 27), it is stated that "nine male animals of every kind are offered; with the blood of these it is their custom to propitiate the gods." Seventy-two animals were counted, but only men, dogs and horses are specifically mentioned: "There (i.e. in the grove, cf. p. 16) hang dogs and horses together with men. One of the Christians told me that he had seen seventy-two of these bodies hanging interspersed[1]." Whatever may have been the original idea of this sacrifice, whether it was intended as an offering of firstlings or not[2], the mention of dogs makes it likely that in Adam's time it was regarded in much the same way as the sacrifice at Leire. Elsewhere the sacrificing of animals together with men does not appear to be mentioned. Yet it is curious that the dog and hawk should be mentioned by Saxo (VIII. p. 414) in connection with the hanging of Broderus. Possibly the story had originally a different form. In Skáldskaparmál 47 and Vǫlsunga s. 40 only the hawk is mentioned. Saxo also states (VIII. p. 411; cf. p. 17 above) that Iarmericus hanged forty Slavs together with wolves, and says further

annos, mense Ianuario, post hoc tempus quo nos theophaniam domini celebramus, omnes conuenerunt et ibi diis suismet xcix. homines et totidem equos cum canibus et gallis pro acciptribus oblatis immolant, pro certo, ut predixi, putantes hos eisdem erga inferos seruituros et commissa crimina apud eosdem placaturos.

[1] Sacrificium itaque tale est. ex omni animante quod masculinum est nouem capita offeruntur, quorum sanguine deos placari mos est......
ibi etiam canes et equi pendent cum hominibus, quorum corpora mixtim suspensa narrauit mihi aliquis christianorum LXXII. uidisse. According to Schol. 137 the sacrifice lasted nine days, one animal of each kind, including a man, being offered every day.

[2] A somewhat similar custom prevailed among the Gauls according to Diodorus v. 32: "They keep their criminals and impale them in sacrifice to the gods every five years, consecrating them with many other offerings and making pyres of immense size." (τοὺς γὰρ κακούργους κατὰ πενταετη-ρίδα φυλάξαντες ἀνασκολοπίζουσι τοῖς θεοῖς καὶ μετ' ἄλλων πολλῶν ἀπαρχῶν καθαγίζουσι, πυρὰς παμμεγέθεις κατασκευάζοντες.)

that this was in early times the punishment for 'parricidium.' It is probable that in these cases the wolf was substituted for the dog in order to disgrace the victim on his arrival in Valhǫll.

Modern writers have been much perplexed by Thietmar's account of the sacrifice at Leire, and it has been suggested that he confused the rites of sacrifice with the funeral ceremonies of the heathen Danes. This supposition seems to me incredible ; the sacrifice at Leire, like that at Upsala, took place every nine years, and the animals sacrificed in both cases included men, horses and dogs. The season, it is true, was different, yet the time of the Leire sacrifice coincides with that of one of the great annual festivals, namely Yule. The true explanation of Thietmar's story is rather to be found in the fact that the funeral rites and the sacrificial rites of the heathen Scandinavians were in great measure identical. Othin is a 'god of the dead' and it is to his abode, Valhǫll ('the hall of the slain'), that the spirits of the dead pass. 'To give to Othin' is to kill; 'to go to Othin' is to die (especially in battle). In the description of the funeral of Haraldr Hilditǫnn in Sǫgubrot af fornkonungum, Haraldr is represented as riding or driving to Valhǫll ; in Saxo's account 'Tartara' is used obviously with the same meaning. So when, in the passage immediately following, Haraldus is to pray Pluto the lord of Orcus (*prestitem Orci Plutonem*), it is clear that this means ' Othin the lord of Valhǫll.' In Saxo II. p. 104 Biarco says : " It is no mean or unknown race, it is not the ashes or the worthless souls of the commons that Pluto seizes ; it is the doom of the mighty which he compasses ; he fills Phlegethon with renowned forms[1]."

[1] Non humile obscurumue genus non funera plebis
Pluto rapit uilesque animas, sed fata potentum
implicat, et claris complet Phlegethonta figuris.

With this may be compared Hárbarðslióð 24 : "Othin possesses the nobles who fall in battle, but Thor has the race of serfs[1]."

Possibly the portraiture of Othin, as he appears in the Sagas, with black cloak and deep-falling hood, is due to his character as god of the dead. There can be no doubt that Thietmar's expression *erga inferos* means "with Othin in Valhǫll.' It appears, at first sight, somewhat singular that these victims, who in late times were as a rule probably either criminals or slaves[2], should be regarded as passing to Valhǫll, and also that they should be provided with horses, dogs and hawks for their use there ; the fact is however capable of explanation. The underlying idea in sacrifice to Othin is that of substitution. King Aun sacrifices his sons to Othin in order that he may have his own life prolonged. King Heiðrekr makes a great slaughter of the Reiðgotar as a ransom to Othin for the life of his son Angantýr (cf. p. 4). A man may save his own life only by giving that of another man, and similarly the state must offer human sacrifices in order to ensure its own preservation and success. The victims may themselves be regarded as worthless, but since they are going to Valhǫll, they must be provided with such articles as are thrown on to the pyre of distinguished warriors. It is quite possible that slaves and criminals were not the persons originally chosen to serve as victims ; from the legendary sagas one would gather that these

---

[1] Óðinn á iarla
þá er í val falla,
en Þórr á þræla kyn.

[2] In a letter to Bonifacius (A.D. 732) Pope Gregorius III. complained that certain Christians were in the habit of selling their slaves to the heathen, who bought them for victims at their sacrifices. Jaffé, Bibliotheca, III. 94.

were frequently selected from a very different class. This change in the status of the human victims seems to harmonise with the fact that apparently no very great care was taken to provide the proper animals, cocks being sacrificed instead of hawks, which were no doubt not so easy to obtain. The change may therefore point to a decay in the vitality of the religion.

In regard to the belief in Valhǫll there are several questions which have not yet been satisfactorily answered. Apparently not all the spirits of the dead were believed to pass thither; indeed if one may judge from the vows of Haraldus, as related by Saxo (cf. p. 7 f.), it would seem that not all even of those who were killed in battle necessarily reached Valhǫll. On the other hand the practice of marking a dying man with a javelin was probably regarded as a substitution for death in battle (cf. p. 13 f.), and thus as conferring the right of admission to Valhǫll. There is no evidence to support the statement quoted above from Hárbarðslióð that the souls of serfs passed to Thor. Thor does not elsewhere appear as a god of the dead, and the statement may perhaps be due to the fact that Thor was especially the god of the lower classes, while Othin was worshipped chiefly, if not solely, by the nobles. Lastly it is not improbable that Valhǫll has been confused to some extent with Ásgarðr ("the court of the *Aesir*"), though originally the two conceptions would seem to have been essentially different. It is noticeable that in the old poetry the terms *Ásgarðr* and *Ásagarðr* occur usually in poems dealing with Thor. Perhaps the doctrine of the "end of the world" was originally connected rather with Ásgarðr than with Valhǫll.

CHAPTER II.

OUTSIDE the limits of the Scandinavian area very few traces of the cult of Woden have been preserved. Yet there is evidence enough to show that the two chief sides of the god's character which are presented in Ynglinga s. 6, 7, namely the crafty, magical, bardic side on the one hand, and the warlike side on the other, were both known to the non-Scandinavian Germans. The first appears from the Latin interpretation (Mercurius) and from the Merseburg magical verses. So also in the Old English Leechdoms (III. 34, 23) Woden is represented as dealing in divination: "then Woden took nine 'twigs of glory' (chips for divination); then he struck the adder so that it flew in nine pieces[1]." It is possible also that the ancient English regarded him as the inventor of the (Runic) alphabet. In the dialogue of Salomon and Saturn the following passage occurs: "Tell me who first invented letters? I tell thee, Mercurius the giant" (*Mercurius se gygand*). It is, of course, possible that the Graeco-Latin god is meant. There is another possible reference in the Runic poem l. 10:—"'Os' is the beginning of every

[1] Ða genam Woden VIIII. wuldortanas, sloh ða ða næddran ðæt heo on VIIII. to fleah.

speech" etc.[1] The meaning of the passage is exceedingly obscure. It is not unlikely that the poem has been revised by some person who did not thoroughly understand his original. In the older poem *os* might have meant Woden. On the other hand Wodan (Woden) as the giver of victory is most clearly depicted in the Langobardic saga (Origo Gentis Langob.; Paulus, Historia Langob. I. 8). In this character he was known also to the English, cf. Ethelwerd II. 2: "the pagans afterwards worshipped Woden as a god with sacrilegious honour, and offered him sacrifice for the acquisition of victory or valour[2]."

Sacrifices to Woden are mentioned by Tacitus (Germ. 9) who states that "they consider it right to sacrifice even human victims to Mercurius on certain fixed days[3]." According to Jonas of Bobbio (Mabillon, Acta sanctorum ord. Bened. II. p. 26) Columbanus (about A.D. 620) found a party of Sueui engaged in "sacrifice" to Wodan. They were sitting round a large vessel full of beer; but the nature of the ceremony is not described. According to Ethelwerd sacrifices were offered by the English to Woden (see above).

The custom of devoting a hostile army to Woden (cf. p. 7) was also known to the continental Germans. The clearest case occurs in Tacitus' description of the war between the Chatti and the Hermunduri (Ann. XIII. 57):—"The war turned out successfully for the Hermunduri, while for the Chatti it was all the more disastrous, because in the event of victory they (i.e. both

[1] os byþ ordfruma ælcre spræce....

[2] Voddan...quem post infanda dignitate ut deum honorantes sacrificium obtulerunt pagani uictoriae causa siue uirtutis.

[3] Deorum maxime Mercurium colunt, cui certis diebus, humanis quoque hostiis litare fas habent.

sides) had dedicated their opponents' army to Mars and Mercurius. By this vow both horses and men, in short everything on the side of the conquered is given up to destruction. And so the threats of our enemies recoiled upon themselves[1]." Another example of the total destruction of an army, which may very well have been due to a vow of this kind, is supplied by Tacitus' account of the scene of Varus' disaster (Ann. I. 61). It seems likely also that the English invaders of Britain practised a similar rite, if one may judge from certain entries in the Saxon Chronicle, especially the entry under the year 491 :—" Ælle and Cissa besieged Anderida and slaughtered all who dwelt therein ; there was not a single Briton left there[2]." It has been mentioned above (p. 7) that amongst the Scandinavians this dedication was symbolized by the casting of a javelin over the enemy's army. Some such idea may have been in the mind of Coifi, the chief priest of the Northumbrians, who according to Bede (H. E. II. 13), as soon as he had given his vote for the change of faith, hurled a spear into the heathen temple. A very early example of the total destruction of a vanquished army in obedience to a vow of this kind is given by Orosius V. 16. After narrating the defeat of Caepio and Mallius by the Cimbri (B.C. 105) he proceeds :—" The enemy captured both camps and acquired an immense quantity of booty. They proceeded to destroy everything which they had captured in accordance with a novel and unusual vow. The clothing was

[1] Sed bellum Hermunduris prosperum, Chattis exitiosius fuit, quia uictores diuersam aciem Marti ac Mercurio sacrauere, quo uoto equi, uiri, cuncta uicta occidioni dantur. et minae quidem hostiles in ipsos uertebant. It is noticeable that the god Mars, i.e. Tiwaz, is here associated with Mercurius (Woden) ; cf. also Orosius VII. 37.

[2] Her Ælle and Cissa ymbsæton Andredes cester and ofslogon alle þa þe þær inne eardedon, ne wearþ þær forþon án Bret to lafe.

torn to shreds and cast away; the gold and silver was
thrown into the river; the corslets of the men were cut
to pieces; the trappings of the horses were broken up;
the horses themselves were drowned in the waters; the
men were hanged on trees, with nooses round their necks.
No booty was allowed to the conqueror and no pity to the
conquered[1]." It is true that the nationality of the
Cimbri and Teutones has not yet been satisfactorily
ascertained. On the whole the evidence is perhaps
somewhat against the supposition that these tribes were
Germanic. Yet there is no doubt that they had lived in
the closest proximity to Germanic tribes, and consequently they may have shared their religious beliefs and
usages. The practice of destroying even the inanimate
property of a vanquished enemy was known among the
Germans of the North at a much later time, probably as
late as the fourth century. This is shown by the immense
quantities of weapons and other articles, which have been
found deposited in the bogs of Thorsbjærg and Nydam
(in Slesvig and South Jutland)[2].

A most singular custom is attributed by Procopius
(Gothic War II. 14) to the Eruli, a tribe which it has
hitherto proved impossible to identify with certainty
with any of the Germanic nations known in later times.
Procopius states simply that they lived formerly beyond
the Danube, but his acquaintance with the geography of
northern Europe was apparently not extensive. The
Eruli are first mentioned in the third century, at which

---

[1] Hostes binis castris atque ingenti praeda potiti noua quadam atque
insolita exsecratione cuncta quae ceperant pessum dederunt: uestis
discissa et proiecta est, aurum argentumque in flumen obiectum, loricae
uirorum concisae, phalerae equorum disperditae, equi ipsi gurgitibus
inmersi, homines laqueis collo inditis ex arboribus suspensi sunt ita ut
nihil praedae uictor, nihil misericordiae uictus adgnosceret.

[2] See Engelhardt, Denmark in the Early Iron Age.

time they appear almost simultaneously on the Black Sea and on the frontier of Gaul. On the whole it seems most probable that their original home was on the southern shores of the Baltic. However this may be, it is quite clear that they were a Germanic tribe and still heathen when part of them were admitted into the Roman empire by Anastasius (A.D. 512). They seem to have been the only important Germanic tribe known to Procopius which had preserved their heathendom till within living memory; for the Goths, Vandals, Gepedes, and Langobardi had long been Christian, and even the Franks were nominally converted before the end of the fifth century, though according to Procopius (G. W. II. 25) they still continued to practise human sacrifices. There seems to be no adequate reason for doubting that the cult of Woden was known to the Eruli. It was certainly practised by all the tribes whose territories lay along the Elbe, the Saxons, Langobardi and Hermunduri; probably also by the Goths whose original home lay far to the East. Procopius simply states that the Eruli worshipped a great number of gods, whom they deemed it right to appease with human sacrifices. There is however some evidence of a different kind (cf. p. 39 f.), which would seem to show that the Eruli had preserved one feature of the cult in a singularly pure form. Procopius' statement about the customs of the Eruli is as follows:—" They had many laws which differed from those of the rest of mankind; for when they became aged or sick they were not allowed to live. As soon as one of them was overtaken by old age or disease it became incumbent on him to request his relatives to put him out of the way as quickly as possible. The relatives made a great pile of logs, reaching to a considerable height, and setting the man on the top they sent up one of the Eruli against him with a dagger. This

man had to be chosen from another family, for it was not
lawful that the executioner should be related to the
victim. And when the man who had been chosen to slay
their kinsman had returned, they proceeded forthwith to
set all the logs on fire, beginning at the extremities of
the pile. When the fire had died out they collected the
bones and buried them without delay in the ground[1]."
Reference has already been made (p. 13 f.) to a custom,
which would seem to have prevailed among the ancient
Scandinavians, of marking a dying man with the point of
a javelin; and it has been pointed out that the passage in
Ynglinga s. 10, in which this rite is described, implies
that it was regarded as a substitution for death in battle.
Now is it possible that this rite was a relic of a still
earlier custom, according to which the dying man was
actually stabbed to death? Such an explanation would
obviously harmonise very well with the purpose of the
rite, and it would be in full accord with the general
conception of Othin and Valhǫll (cf. p. 26 f.). Then the
custom attributed to the Eruli at the end of the fifth or
beginning of the sixth century will represent simply an
earlier stage in the history of the same rite. It is true
that the weapon used by the Eruli is stated to have been
a dagger and not a javelin; but a discrepancy in such a
detail as this may be due to inaccuracy on the part of

---

[1] νόμοις δὲ πολλοῖς οὐ κατὰ ταὐτὰ τοῖς ἄλλοις ἀνθρώποις ἐχρῶντο. οὔτε γὰρ
γηράσκουσιν οὔτε νοσοῦσιν αὐτοῖς βιοτεύειν ἐξῆν, ἀλλ' ἐπειδάν τις αὐτῶν ἢ
γήρᾳ ἢ νόσῳ ἀλῴη ἐπάναγκές οἱ ἐγίνετο τοὺς ξυγγενεῖς αἰτεῖσθαι ὅτι τάχιστα ἐξ
ἀνθρώπων αὐτὸν ἀφανίζειν. οἱ δὲ ξύλα πολλὰ ἐς μέγα τι ὕψος ξυννήσαντες
καθίσαντές τε τὸν ἄνθρωπον ἐν τῇ τῶν ξύλων ὑπερβολῇ τῶν τινα Ἐρούλων
ἀλλότριον μέντοι σὺν ξιφιδίῳ παρ' αὐτὸν ἔπεμπον. ξυγγενῆ γὰρ αὐτῷ τὸν
φονέα εἶναι οὐ θέμις. ἐπειδὰν δὲ αὐτοῖς ὁ τοῦ ξυγγενοῦς φονεὺς ἐπανῄει,
ξύμπαντα ἔκαιον αὐτίκα τὰ ξύλα, ἐκ τῶν ἐσχάτων ἀρξάμενοι. παυσαμένης τε
αὐτοῖς τῆς φλογὸς ξυλλέξαντες τὰ ὀστᾶ τὸ παραυτίκα τῇ γῇ ἔκρυπτον. (For
the continuation of this passage see p. 41.)

Procopius. Examples of voluntary death in the Scandinavian legends are rare. Yet there are two cases of special significance: Hadingus, a hero who frequently appears under Othin's protection, commits suicide by hanging himself (Saxo I. p. 60)[1], and Starcatherus, the foster-son of Othin and his typical hero, requests and receives death at the hand of Hatherus (Saxo VIII. p. 405 f.). In the latter case the killing is done with a sword. A singular custom of killing the old is mentioned in Gautreks s. 1, 2 (F. A. S. III. p. 7 ff.). The victims suffered voluntarily; man and wife were put to death together by being thrown over a precipice. Among the Germans of the Continent, there is, so far as I am aware, no evidence for any such custom beyond the passage quoted above from Procopius. Tacitus only says (Germ. 6) that persons who have succeeded in making their escape after a disastrous battle, and have lost their shields in so doing, frequently strangle themselves to death, and so put an end to their dishonour[2]. With this passage may be compared Ragnars s. Loðbrókar c. 9 (F. A. S. I. 261 ff.), where the defeated Eirekr son of Ragnar is offered full freedom and favour by king Eysteinn, yet prefers to be killed (probably as a sacrifice). The survivors of the Cimbri also killed themselves after the battle of Vercellae according to Plutarch (Marius 27, see below), and their wives followed their example. The same was the case with the women of the Teutones after the battle of Aquae Sextiae (Florus III. 3; Hieronymus, Ep. ad Ageruchiam).

Very little is known of the ritual practised by the ancient

---

[1] It is perhaps worth calling to mind that Hadingus was probably, in origin, identical with Niǫrðr. Saxo's account of Hadingus' suicide may therefore have some bearing on the passage in Ynglinga s. 11, which states that "Niǫrðr had himself marked for Othin."

[2] Multique superstites bellorum infamiam laqueo finierunt.

Germans in their human sacrifices¹.   The general employment of hanging however as a means of capital punishment
renders it probable that this was at least one of the methods
practised.   According to Tacitus (Germ. 12) "traitors and
deserters were hanged on trees," while cowards and others
were suffocated in marshes.   The officers of Varus' army,
according to Tacitus (Ann. I. 61) were "slaughtered at
the altars"; some of the troops appear to have been
buried alive, others possibly were hanged².   The custom
of hanging captured enemies was certainly known to the
Goths.   Thus according to Jordanes (c. 48) the Ostro-
gothic king Vinitharius, in order to strike terror into the
Anti, hanged their king Boz with his sons and seventy of
their nobles³.   Hanging seems to have been much practised by the Cimbri.   In Orosius' account of the Roman
disaster on the Rhone, the Roman captives are stated to
have been hanged on the trees (cf. p. 31 f.).   After their
defeat at Vercellae, according to Plutarch (Marius 27),
the fugitives attempted to hang themselves by any means
that lay ready to hand :—"As there were no trees at
hand the men tied their necks, some to the horns and
some to the legs of the oxen; then they applied goads to
the oxen and, as the latter rushed off, they were dragged
along and crushed, and thus met their death⁴."   According to the same chapter (cf. Florus III. 3) the women also
either hanged or strangled themselves.   The expression

¹ Cf. Golther, Mythologie 561 ff.
² If *patibula* is here used for 'gallows.'
³ This story affords a curious confirmation to Saxo's account of
Iarmericus.   According to Jord. 14 Vinitharius was the great-nephew of
Hermanaricus (Iarmericus).   Vinitharius would seem to have reigned
towards the end of the fourth century.
⁴ τοὺς δ᾽ ἄνδρας ἀπορίᾳ δένδρων τοῖς κέρασι τῶν βοῶν τοὺς δὲ τοῖς σκέλεσι
προσδεῖν αὐτῶν τραχήλους· εἶτα κέντρα προσφέροντας ἐξαλλομένων τῶν βοῶν
ἐφελκομένους καὶ πατουμένους ἀπόλλυσθαι.

ἀπορίᾳ δένδρων "through lack of trees" deserves consideration, because it distinctly implies the existence of
some suicidal rite in which tree-hanging formed an
essential feature. There is not however sufficient evidence
for determining whether the rite was practised generally
or only under special conditions. It is conceivable, for
instance, that some vow had been made which involved
death in case of defeat. On the other hand it is possible
that the Cimbri, like the later Eruli, held it unlawful to
die a natural death; consequently, when all hope of
further successful fighting was gone, sacrificial suicide was
the only course left open.

The allusions to the prevalence of hanging among the
Cimbri are so frequent that there can be little doubt that
they practised either the cult of Woden or at least some
cult which employed very similar rites. An account of
their methods of sacrifice is given by Strabo (VII. p. 294).
"Their women accompanied them on their march and
were attended by holy prophetesses with gray hair and
white clothing. These had linen mantles fastened by a
buckle, bronze girdles and bare feet. When prisoners
were brought into the camp, they met them sword in
hand and, after consecrating them, they led them to a
bronze bowl, capable of holding about twenty amphorae.
They had a ladder on which she climbed...[1]. Standing
above the bowl she cut each man's throat as he hung
suspended. They practised divination from the blood as
it gushed out into the bowl. Others slit them asunder
and disembowelled them, proclaiming victory to their own
people[2]." With the last sentence may be compared the

---

[1] The text is corrupt here.

[2] ...ταῖς γυναιξὶν αὐτῶν συστρατευούσαις παρηκολούθουν προμάντεις ἱέρειαι
πολιότριχες, λευχείμονες, καρπασίνας ἐφαπτίδας ἐπιπεπορπημέναι, ζῶσμα
χαλκοῦν ἔχουσαι, γυμνόποδες· τοῖς οὖν αἰχμαλώτοις διὰ τοῦ στρατοπέδου

Scandinavian rite of cutting the "blood-eagle" (cf. p. 20), which is represented in Orkneyinga s. 8 as a sacrifice to Othin for victory. It is noticeable that in these Cimbric sacrifices, as in the sacrifice of Vikar (cf. p. 3 f.), hanging and stabbing seem to be combined, though it is not stated that the hanging was of such a nature as in itself to cause death. For the combination of sacrifice with divination Scandinavian parallels can be found, though I am not aware that there is any evidence for the practice of divination at human sacrifices[1]. It ought to be mentioned however that a rite still more closely resembling that of the Cimbri is attributed by Diodorus (v. 31) to the Gauls.

The Old English poem Beowulf has already been quoted (p. 18) in illustration of the Scandinavian custom of hanging captured enemies. The same poem contains apparently an allusion to another very curious custom, whether English or Scandinavian is not clear. After describing how Herebeald, son of Hreðel king of the Geatas, was accidentally killed by his brother Hæðcyn, the poem goes on to describe the grief of Hreðel, concluding as follows (l. 2444 ff.):—"Thus it is grievous for an old man to endure, that his young son should ride on the gallows. Then shall he utter a dirge, a sorrowful song, when his son hangs, a joy to the raven, and he himself, aged and experienced as he is, can not help him or serve

συνήντων ξιφήρεις, καταστέψασαι δ᾽ αὐτοὺς ἦγον ἐπὶ κρατῆρα χαλκοῦν ὅσον ἀμφορέων εἴκοσιν· εἶχον δὲ ἀναβάθραν ἣν ἀναβᾶσα......ὑπερπετὴς τοῦ λέβητος ἐλαιμοτόμει ἕκαστον μετεωρισθέντα· ἐκ δὲ τοῦ προχεομένου αἵματος εἰς τὸν κρατῆρα μαντείαν τινὰ ἐποιοῦντο, ἄλλαι δὲ διασχίσασαι ἐσπλάγχνευον ἀναφθεγγόμεναι νίκην τοῖς οἰκείοις.

[1] Is it possible that the obscure verse (155) of Hávamál, quoted above (p. 19), should contain a reminiscence of some such rite as this? It is perhaps worth recalling that human blood is contained in the vessel Óðrerir, from which comes the gift of poetry (cf. Bragræður 57).

him in any way[1]." There is no indication that the person hanged was a criminal, and the context does not admit of the supposition that he had been captured in war. It is not quite clear how far the passage is intended as a simile. If the poet is thinking of Herebeald in l. 2445—6, it would seem to show that the bodies of dead persons were hung on the gallows. Otherwise it must be inferred that he was acquainted with some custom similar to that practised by the Eruli (p. 33 f.), though in this case death was brought about by hanging.

It has been mentioned (p. 21) that the invention of the "wedge" order of battle was ascribed to Othin by the Scandinavians. There is no evidence for the existence of such a belief among the continental Germans. The "wedge" however was well known and was recognized even in the very earliest times as the Germans' favourite method of warfare (cf. Caesar, B. G. I. 52; Tacitus, Germ. 6). It has also been suggested in explanation of Ynglinga s. 6, that the typical Othin-worshipper in early times was a light-armed warrior. Now the Germans of the first century were certainly light-armed, their favourite weapon being the javelin. Tacitus' statements (Germ. 6) convey the impression that this was due to their inability to procure defensive armour. Such however can not have been the case with the Eruli in later times, for this tribe appears to have continued to practise light-armed warfare at a time when all the neighbouring tribes were well provided with defensive armour. Jordanes (c. 23) states that " at

Customs in war associated with the cult of Woden.

---

[1] swa bi‍ð geomorlic gomelum ceorle
to gebidanne, þæt his byre ride
giong on galgan : þonne he gyd wrece,
sarigne sang, þonne his sunu hangað
hrefne to hroðre and he him helpan ne mæg,
eald and infrod ænige gefremman.

that time (i.e. in the fourth century) there was no nation
which did not possess in its army a body of light-armed
troops selected from among the Eruli[1]." In his account
of the battle between the Huns and Gepidæ (Gepedes) he
compares the light equipment of the Eruli with the heavy
armour of the Alani (c. 50). The equipment of the Eruli
is described by Procopius (Persian War, II. 25) as follows:
"The Eruli wear neither helmet nor coat of mail nor any
other protection except a shield and a thick cloak; girded
with this they proceed to battle[2]." He adds that their
slaves fought even without shields. Procopius' statement
is corroborated by Paulus (Hist. Langobard. I. 20):—"At
that time (about the end of the fifth century) the Eruli
were experienced in the arts of war and had acquired
great glory by the slaughter of many nations. Whether
for the sake of fighting with greater freedom, or to show
their contempt for any wound inflicted by the enemy,
they used to fight unprotected, covering only the loins[3]."
This absence of defensive armour is probably to be ascribed
to the conservative instincts of the tribe, backed by the
sanction of their religion.

In Ynglinga s. 10 Othin is stated to have instituted
Funeral customs associated with the cult of Woden. the custom of cremation, and to have declared
that every man should possess in Valhǫll the
property which had been burnt with him on
his pyre (cf. p. 22). Cremation was practised
by the ancient Germans in the time of Tacitus (Germ. 27)

---

[1] Nulla siquidem erat tunc gens quae non leuem armaturam in acie
sua ex ipsis eligeret.

[2] οὔτε γὰρ κράνος οὔτε θώρακα οὔτε ἄλλο τι φυλακτήριον Ἐρουλοι ἔχουσιν
ὅτι μὴ ἀσπίδα καὶ τριβώνιον ἀδρὸν ὃ δὴ διεζωσμένοι ἐς τὸν ἀγῶνα καθίστανται.

[3] Erant siquidem tunc Heroli bellorum usibus exerciti multorumque
iam strage notissimi. qui siue ut expeditius bella gererent siue ut inlatum
ab hoste uulnus contemnerent, nudi pugnabant, operientes solummodo
corporis uerecunda.

and continued long after, though it had apparently been
given up by the Franks before their conversion. It was
practised, at least partly, by the English after their con-
quest of Britain, and by the Eruli until the beginning of
the sixth century (cf. p. 33 f.). By the Old Saxons it seems
to have been practised even towards the end of the eighth
century. It was prohibited by an edict of Karl the Great
in 785[1]. Tacitus seems to have been struck by the
simplicity of the German funeral rites. He states that
they had no monuments except a mound covered with
grass. Yet he adds that weapons and in some cases horses
were thrown on to the pyre. The funeral customs of the
ancient Germans therefore did not differ essentially from
those practised in the North. Procopius however (Gothic
War, II. 14; cf. p. 33 f.) distinctly states that suttee was
practised by the Eruli :—" When a man of the Eruli dies,
it becomes incumbent on his widow, if she makes any
claim to virtue and wishes to leave behind her a good
reputation, to strangle herself to death without much
delay beside her husband's tomb. If she does not do this,
she forfeits all respect for the rest of her life and incurs
the enmity of her husband's relatives[2]." This is, so far
as I am aware, the only passage in which the practice of
suttee is attributed to any Germanic tribe[3]. Yet a careful

[1] Capitula quae de partibus Saxoniae constituta sunt; c. 7: si quis
corpus defuncti hominis secundum ritum paganorum flamma consumi
fecerit et ossa eius ad cinerem redegerit, capite punietur. (Pertz, M. G.
III. 49.)

[2] Ἐρούλου δὲ ἀνδρὸς τελευτήσαντος ἐπάναγκες τῇ γυναικὶ ἀρετῆς μεταποιου-
μένῃ καὶ κλέος αὐτῇ ἐθελούσῃ λείπεσθαι βρόχον ἀναψαμένῃ παρὰ τὸν τοῦ
ἀνδρὸς τάφον οὐκ εἰς μακρὸν θνήσκειν. οὐ ποιούσῃ δὲ ταῦτα περιειστήκει τὸ
λοιπὸν ἀδόξῳ τε εἶναι καὶ τοῖς τοῦ ἀνδρὸς ξυγγενέσι προσκεκρουκέναι.

[3] It is clear that the custom was known to the western Slavs down to
comparatively late times. It is mentioned by Bonifacius in A.D. 745 (Ep.
72; ad Ethilbaldum reg. Merc.), and is stated by Thietmar of Merseburg

examination of the northern legends will reveal the fact
that some such custom was not altogether unknown amongst
the ancient Scandinavians. According to Saxo I. p. 46
Gunnilda, the wife of Asmundus, refused to survive her
husband's death and took her life, apparently with a sword.
In Vǫlsunga s. 8 (F.A.S. I. 135) Signý prefers to die with
her husband Siggeir, though she has brought his death
about and killed the children which he had by her. In
Gylfaginning 49 Nanna is represented as dying of grief at
Balder's pyre; possibly in an earlier version of the story
she committed suicide. In Hervarar s. 5 (F.A.S. I. 429)
Ingibiǫrg, daughter of Yngvi (or Ingialdr) king of the
Swedes, is represented as hearing of the death of Hialmar,
to whom she was betrothed. What follows is differently
related in different texts; according to one text "she was
so much affected by Hialmar's fall that she straightway
died of grief[1];" according to another "the king's daughter
can not bear to survive him and determines to put an end
to her own life[2]." The case of Brynhildr may also be
quoted (cf. Sigurðarkviða in skamma; Vǫlsunga s. 31).
Brynhildr was not the wife of Sigurðr, though she had
desired that position. After bringing about Sigurðr's
death she kills herself with a sword (Sigurðarkv. 48), and
gives directions that she is to be burnt with Sigurðr
(cf. p. 23). In the poem Helreið Brynhildar she is represented as driving to Valhǫll. The poem concludes with
the words "Sigurðr and I shall never part again[3]."

(VIII. 2) to have been in general use among the Poles during the latter
part of the tenth century.

[1] fékk henni svá mikils fall Hialmars at hún sprakk þegar af harmi
etc.

[2] en konungs dóttir má eigi lifa eptir hann ok ræðr sér siálf bana.

[3] vit skulum okkrum
aldri slíta
Sigurðr saman. (v. 14.)

Another example, dating from curiously late times, is preserved by Jakut under the article Rus (quoted by J. Grimm, kl. Schriften II. p. 289 ff.). A certain Ibn Fazlan, who records the story, witnessed the funeral of a noble Russian on the lower Volga, about the year 922—3. The dead man was burnt on a ship in the river. Various animals were killed and thrown on to the pyre, a dog, a cock and hen (possibly in the place of hawks, cf. p. 24), two horses and two oxen. A young woman was also killed and laid beside the dead man. It appears from Ibn Fazlan's account that she was not the wife of the dead man, but chosen from among his concubines. These were asked which of them was willing to die with their master· The offer was voluntary, but when once made, could not be retracted. The method of killing employed was a combination of strangling and stabbing, the latter being carried out by an old woman who was known as the "death's-angel." J. Grimm (l.c. p. 294) did not believe that these people were Scandinavians. His objections however do not seem to have been sufficiently well grounded. Ibn Fazlan distinguishes clearly between the Russians and the Slavs. That the "Russians" were Scandinavians is rendered probable by the fact that according to Constantinus Porphyrogenitus (On the Administration of the Empire, c. 9) the Russians and Slavs spoke different languages (Ρωσιστί, Σκλαβινιστί), the former of which was, to judge from his examples, undoubtedly Scandinavian[1]. The ship-funeral also, as related

[1] For further evidence to the same effect cf. Zeuss, die Deutschen u. die Nachbarstämme, p. 547 ff. The story of the 'Russians,' who were sent by the eastern emperor Theophilus to the emperor Ludwig in 839, especially deserves consideration : *misit etiam* (Theophilus) *cum eis quosdam, qui se, id est gentem suam, Rhos uocari dicebant......quorum aduentus causam imperator* (i.e. Ludwig) *diligentius inuestigans, comperit eos gentis esse Sueonum* etc.

by Ibn Fazlan seems to be a distinctively Scandinavian custom. At the same time some doubt may be expressed as to whether the practice of suttee was at all common at this late period. Lastly reference may be made to a custom attributed by Bonifacius (Ep. 72, written A.D. 745) to the Old Saxons:—"In Old Saxony if a maiden brings disgrace upon her father's house by unchastity, they sometimes compel her to put an end to her life by hanging herself with her own hand. Her body is then laid on the pyre and cremated, and the partner of her guilt is hanged over her tomb[1]." A close parallel to this passage is afforded by Saxo's account of Hagbarthus and Sygne (VII. p. 343 ff.), a legend to which frequent reference is made in Scandinavian poetry. Hagbarthus had made his way in woman's attire to the abode of Sygne, daughter of the Danish king Sigarus. There he was arrested and condemned to death, partly on account of seducing Sygne, but partly also because he had killed two of Sigarus' sons in battle. Sygne decides to share Hagbarthus' fate and begs her handmaidens to die with her. They pile faggots against the walls of the room and make halters of their robes. When Hagbarthus is led to the gallows, he asks that his coat may first be hanged, in order that he may test Sygne's constancy. When this is notified to Sygne, whose room is some distance from the place of execution, she and her maidens, thinking that Hagbarthus is already dead, set fire to the room and push away the beams on which they were standing, thus hanging themselves. Hagbarthus, seeing the flames, meets his fate with joy. It is to be noticed that Sygne's death is entirely voluntary. Among

[1] Nam in antiqua Saxonia si uirgo paternam domum cum adulterio maculauerit, aliquando cogunt eam propria manu per laqueum suspensam uitam finire et super bustum illius incensae et concrematae corruptorem eius suspendunt.

the Old Saxons on the other hand the woman was compelled to die, but stress is certainly to be laid on the
words *propria manu*. She was not executed but compelled
to commit suicide. The practice seems therefore to have
been associated in some way with the idea of suttee. It
is worth noticing also that in both cases the man is put
to death by hanging. Lastly the case of the Teutones
and Cimbri may be quoted. It is stated by several
authors (Florus, III. 3; Plutarch, Mar. 27; Hieronymus,
Ep. ad Ageruchiam) that after the battles of Aquae
Sextiae and Vercellae the women of these tribes, after
vainly attempting resistance, first destroyed their children
and then put themselves to death, chiefly by hanging,
some even using their hair for this purpose. Florus and
Hieronymus indeed state that they first made an application to Marius for freedom and permission to exercise
their sacerdotal office, and that they put themselves to
death only when this application had failed. It would
appear however that this application was only made by a
small number, three hundred according to Hieronymus.
These were perhaps the prophetesses mentioned by Strabo
(VII. p. 294; cf. p. 37 above).

These examples are enough to show that suttee, or
some very similar custom, was known to various Germanic
tribes from very early times. Procopius' statement is
therefore not without foundation. Whether Tacitus means
to refer to any such custom in Germania 18 f. is not quite
clear. One may be tempted to connect the existence of
this rite with the strict views which, according to Tacitus,
the ancient Germans entertained on matrimony. On the
other hand it may also have had a very different origin.
It might, for example, have arisen from the idea that the
wife was part of the husband's property, and consequently
required by him, together with his horses, dogs and hawks,

in order to complete his happiness in the next world.
The latter explanation is favoured by the fact that the
woman killed was apparently not always the man's lawful
wife. Against this it may perhaps be objected that it is
inconsistent with the Germanic conception of marriage.
Yet it has still to be proved that the cult of Woden is of
Germanic origin. If the cult was introduced from abroad,
the same may also be true of such a rite as this; for,
since the rite undoubtedly presupposes a belief in a certain
kind of immortality, it may very well have been connected,
even from the beginning, with the cult of Woden.

Notwithstanding the paucity of the evidence, there
seems to be every reason for believing that the
cult of Woden, as practised by the continental
Germans in the earliest historical times, cor-
responded to the Scandinavian cult in all its
essential features. It is clear: (1) that human
victims were sacrificed to Woden; (2) that in war the
enemy were sometimes dedicated to Woden, a vow which
involved the slaughter of all prisoners and the destruction
of all the booty; (3) that such prisoners were often put to
death by hanging. The frequent occurrence of hanging
as a method of punishment suggests also that human
victims were regularly sacrificed to Othin in this way,
but conclusive evidence is wanting. Perhaps hanging
and stabbing were combined, as appears to have been
the case with the Cimbri (cf. p. 37 f.). For the sacrificial
use of the javelin there is hardly sufficient evidence,
though it is to be remembered that this was the favourite
weapon of the ancient Germans. Further it is clear (4)
that certain Germanic tribes (at all events the Eruli)
practised a method of warfare which showed a reckless
contempt of danger and has some resemblance to the
"berserksgangr" of the North; (5) that the funeral rites

*Conclu-
sion. The
application
of the
foregoing
evidence to
the Scandi-
navian cult.*

practised by the ancient Germans seem to have closely resembled those which in the North were associated with the cult of Othin. Suttee, or some very similar custom, seems to have been known both on the continent and in the North. In all these points the Scandinavian and continental cults agree. In one respect the continental cult, at all events, as practised by the Eruli, seems to have had a more primitive and barbarous form. Men were not allowed to die by disease or old age, but had to be despatched by violence on the approach of death. In the North on the other hand this act seems to be represented by a merely formal stabbing. It is possible however that in very early times the dying man was actually killed (cf. p. 34 f.).

It is clear that the Eruli worshipped a "god of the dead," and it is very probable that the Cimbri practised a cult of the same kind. That this god was Woden is rendered probable by the fact that he was the recipient of human sacrifices, and also by the "dedication" vow, though in this case he seems to have been associated with "Mars." Some conception answering to that of the Scandinavian Valhǫll must therefore have prevailed among the ancient Germans. Since the poetry of heathen times is entirely lost, it is no wonder that this conception can not now be traced. Possibly we owe to it such expressions as the O.E. *neorxna wang* = paradisus. The word *walcyrge* (*wælcyrie*) is also of frequent occurrence in the Old English glossaries, but from the words which it is used to gloss (*Erinys, Tisiphona, Bellona* etc.), as also from its frequent appearance in the phrase *wiccean and wælcyrian*, it would seem to have had a different meaning from the Norse *valkyria*. Since there can be little doubt that the latter is in great measure a creation of the Scandinavian poets, it is not unlikely that the English usage may reflect an earlier conception. Possibly the word originally denoted the "promantis," who sacrificed human victims and practised divination from their blood[1]. The transference of the valkyrie from the earthly sphere to Valhǫll will in that case be a later development. It cannot, of course, be denied that the English *walcyrge* had supernatural features, but these appear rather to have been of the werwolf class.

[1] Cf. the 'death's angel' in Ibn Fazlan's story (p. 43).

CHAPTER III.

SINCE the appearance of H. Petersen's book, Om Nordboernes Gudekyrkelse og Gudetro i Hedenold (1876), it has been generally agreed that the cult of Othin was not indigenous in the North. The date of its introduction is however very difficult to fix, even approximately. Among recent writers Golther (Mythologie, p. 223) holds that this took place at all events before 800 ; while Mogk (Paul's Grundriss, I. p. 1070) believes that it came to the Saxons before they settled in Britain (in the fifth century), and passed over to the North, not much later, by way of Denmark; Othin however did not become the central point of the Northern mythology before the Viking Age (ib. p. 1063). By an examination of all the available evidence it might perhaps be possible to arrive at a somewhat more definite result.

1. *The name " Othin " (Óðinn, from earlier * Wōðenaz).*

It is clear that this word must have become known to the Scandinavians at a time when the loss of the sound w- before labial vowels had not yet ceased to operate. The loss of this sound brought about the disuse of the letter w in the Runic alphabet. For the name of the

c. 4

letter was probably *wunju (cf. O.E. wyn), which later became sounded *unju[1]; the letter u therefore took the place of w. The earliest certain example of this substitution occurs in the inscription of Kallerup, which has the form suiþks for swiðings. A probable example of the sound-change is supplied by the form urti in the inscription of Sölvesborg[2]. Wimmer dates the inscription of Sölvesborg at about 750—775 and that of Kallerup at about 800—825. I am under the impression that Wimmer's dating of the inscriptions is in all cases somewhat too late. In the present case however that is of little importance. The loss of the sound w- took place at all events after the syncope of final -a, and this latter change is not likely to have taken place before the beginning of the sixth century, and may be somewhat later. The word Óðinn therefore can not prove the existence of the cult before the sixth century at the earliest.

2. The legends of Othin-heroes.

The antiquity of some of these legends is shown by their appearance in Beowulf, a poem which deals almost exclusively with Scandinavian affairs. Beowulf's acquaintance with Scandinavian history does not extend to events which happened later than the first half of the sixth century, and it may be assumed with a certain amount of probability that legends, which appear in the poem, were already current by this time either among the English or among some of the Northern peoples.

[1] The regular form in the later language would be *yn, but the word is lost.

[2] The right reading may however be Ruti.

i. The story of Sigmundr, son of Vǫlsungr. It has long been recognised that the cult of Othin is an essential feature in the history of the Vǫlsung family (cf. Müllenhoff, Z. f. d. A. XXIII. 116 ff.). This is true above all in the case of Sigmundr. Othin gives Sigmundr a sword with which he is always victorious until his last battle, when the sword breaks on Othin's javelin (cf. p. 16). In the Eireksmál Sigmundr is represented, together with Sinfiǫtli (his son by his son Signý), as welcoming Eirekr at the gates of Valhǫll. Reference is made in Beowulf (875 ff.) to legends about Sigemund and Fitela (i.e. Sinfiǫtli), though it is stated only that the latter was the son of Sigemund's sister[1], not of Sigemund himself. The evidence is however hardly conclusive for proving that Othin-heroes were known to the Danes at this time; for Beowulf is an English poem, and the legend, which seems not to have been Scandinavian originally, might have been known to the poet before it came to the Danes.

ii. Hermóðr. This hero is mentioned together with Sigmundr in Hyndlulióð 2 :—" He (Othin) gave Hermóðr a helmet and coat of mail, and Sigmundr a sword[2]." Hermóðr therefore, like Sigmundr, appears to have been under Othin's special protection. In Hákonarmál Hermóðr together with Bragi welcomes Hákon at the gates of Valhǫll, discharging therefore the duty which in Eireksmál is allotted to Sigmundr. Legends about this hero must once have existed, but now his name is only known from these two passages. It is unnecessary for the present purpose to discuss the question whether he is

---

[1] l. 881. eam his nefan.

[2] gaf hann Hermóði
hiálm ok bryniu
en Sigmundi
sverð at þiggia.

really identical with the god Hermóðr, who is mentioned
in the account of Balder's death (Gylf. 49). The latter
seems to be the Hermóðr, to whom reference is made in
Sǫgubrot af fornkonungum 3 (F. A. S. I. 373). It is
noticeable that in both the passages in which his name
occurs, Hermóðr is associated, either directly or implicitly,
not only with Othin but also with Sigmundr. Now in
Beowulf, 898 ff., Sigemund is compared with a certain
Heremod, who, like Hermóðr, appears to have been a
great warrior. Since the names Hermóðr and Heremód
are identical, and both occur in conjunction with Sig-
mundr-Sigemund, it is very probable that they denote
the same person. In that case there is evidence in
Beowulf for the existence of another Othin-hero. This
case also is not open to the same objection as that of
Sigmundr, for it is quite clear from Beowulf 913, 1709 ff.,
that Heremod was regarded as a Danish king, though
belonging to a past generation.

iii. Starkaðr. This hero was regarded by the Danes
as the typical servant of Othin (cf. p. 71). His story has
acquired mythological features, but there seems to be a
certain amount of historical foundation for that part of
his career, in which he is associated with the Danish
kings Fróði (Frotho) and Ingialdr (Ingellus). Now the
episode in which Starcatherus incites Ingellus to murder
the sons of Suertingus (Saxo VI. pp. 303—315), cannot be
separated from Beowulf's account of the old warrior (*eald
œscwiga*), who goads Ingeld into revenge (2041 ff.). The
warrior's name is not mentioned in Beowulf, but there can
be little doubt that he is identical with Starcatherus. His
position differs from that of Sigemund and Heremod in
that he is represented as a contemporary of Beowulf,
while the others are already heroes of the past. He
belongs to the Heaðobeardnas, a tribe which has not been

successfully identified; yet since Frotho and Ingellus appear in Saxo as Danish kings, it is probable that the Heaðobeardnas were nothing more than a division of the Danes, and that their war with the Scyldingas was dynastic rather than national. It is impossible to suppose that Starcatherus (Starkaðr) was regarded by Saxo and the Norse writers otherwise than as a Scandinavian hero. It is to be observed also that in Saxo Starcatherus is not represented as the introducer of a new cult, but, on the contrary, as an essentially conservative character. It is reasonable therefore to suppose that the cult of Othin was in existence before his time.

On the whole therefore the acquaintance of Beowulf with the Othin-heroes Sigmundr and Hermóðr, and with a person who seems at a later time to have developed into the Othin-hero Starkaðr, renders it probable that the cult of Othin was already known to the Danes in the first half of the sixth century.

3. The institutions and customs associated with the cult of Othin.

i. Sacrificial hanging. It has been shown that the custom of hanging is known to Beowulf both in the case of enemies captured in war (cf. p. 18), and apparently also in cases of natural or accidental death (cf. p. 38 f.). In the former case the practice is attributed to the Swedish king Ongentheo, whose death, judging from Beowulf, would seem to have taken place about the end of the fifth century. It has further been pointed out (p. 17 f.) that the practice of hanging, as a distinctly sacrificial act, is attributed to the Scandinavians by Procopius, who says that human victims are sacrificed in this and other ways to "Ares." It has often been supposed that the god here meant is Týr ; but there is little evidence in favour of such an assumption. Týr is an unimportant figure in the northern mythology, and there is no record of human sacrifices being offered to him. The sacrifice by hanging is never mentioned in connection with any other god than Othin, Thor's victims being put to death in an entirely different manner (cf. p. 19). That "Ares" might be used for Othin is shown, not only by the fact that Othin was regarded as the giver of victory, but also by Saxo's use of "Mars" in the same sense (cf. p. 18, n. 3). Procopius' information was perhaps derived from those Eruli who had been in "Thule." Together with the passage from Beowulf quoted above, his account renders it probable that the cult of Othin was practised in the North about the beginning of the sixth century.

ii. Weapons and tactics in warfare. There is a very strong resemblance between the method of warfare attributed to Othin's heroes in Ynglinga s. 6 and the method practised by the Eruli in the sixth century (cf. p. 39 f.). In its main features also this method of warfare seems to have resembled that practised by the ancient Germans of Tacitus' time. The absence of defensive armour is a distinctive feature in all these cases. Further the "wedge" formation, which was greatly practised by the ancient Germans, was believed by the Scandinavians to be an invention of Othin's (cf. p. 21). Among the ancient Germans the absence of defensive armour is in all probability to be attributed to the difficulty experienced in obtaining it. With the Eruli of the fifth and sixth centuries this can hardly have been the case; their reluctance to use armour must have been based, at least in part, on religious grounds (cf. p. 40). This association however between religion and the custom of fighting unprotected would rather seem to show that the cult had been known at a time when defensive armour had not yet come into use. Now, if, on the same principle, we are justified in assuming that the equipment attributed to Othin's heroes in Ynglinga saga shows that, at the time when the cult was introduced, defensive armour was still unknown, then the introduction of the cult can hardly be dated later than the beginning of the fifth century. For the discoveries at Thorsbjærg and Nydam (cf. p. 62) show that both the helmet and coat of mail were known to the inhabitants of Slesvig and southern Jutland during the fourth century, and also that by the same time the sword and the long spear had, to a great extent, taken the place of the javelin. Weapons used in Slesvig during the fourth century could hardly fail to be known in Sweden within the space of another hundred years[1].

Lastly it perhaps deserves notice that the "runes" are frequently mentioned in connection with Othin, not merely in the sense of "mysteries," but also as denoting the written characters. There seem to be traces of a similar association of ideas amongst the ancient English (cf. p. 29). Unfortunately however the age of the Runic inscriptions in the North is still a matter of dispute. On the whole it seems probable that the oldest inscriptions of Sweden and Norway are not later than the fifth century. This however gives no indication of the date at which writing was introduced. It is not likely that a single inscription in England dates from within a hundred and fifty years of the first invasion; there are only two which have any

---

[1] The argument is, of course, not conclusive. The description of Othin's equipment might also be due to a tradition imported from abroad simultaneously with the cult. The latter explanation would seem to necessitate the belief that the ritual use of the javelin was acquired together with the cult.

reasonable claim to be dated before A.D. 650. The case of the so-called "tree-runes" may be compared. There can be little doubt that they are pan-Germanic; yet there is no certain example of their use in the North until late in the Viking age. Hence even if none of the extant Runic inscriptions prove to be earlier than the beginning of the sixth century, it is likely enough that the alphabet was known two or three centuries earlier.

The results of this discussion may be briefly summarised as follows: There is good reason, from several different sides, for believing that the cult of Othin was known in the North at the beginning of the sixth century; the positive evidence for proving an acquaintance with the cult before this time is not strong; but on the other hand there is no evidence whatever to the contrary.

In Tacitus' account the Swedes (Suiones) present a

Tacitus' account of the Swedes.

striking contrast to all the other nations of Germany. After describing the construction of their ships he proceeds (Germ. 44):—"These people pay respect even to wealth. The power is therefore vested in one man. Here there are no reservations; his claim to obedience does not rest merely on sufferance. Nor are weapons to be seen in every man's hand, as is the case with the rest of the Germans. On the contrary they are kept stored away in the charge of a slave[1]." The state of society here depicted is clearly incompatible with the existence of such a cult as that of Othin, which could hardly flourish except under conditions of chronic warfare[2]. On the other hand it corresponds excellently with

[1] Est apud illos et opibus honos; eoque unus imperitat, nullis iam exceptionibus, non precario iure parendi. nec arma, ut apud ceteros Germanos, in promiscuo, sed clausa sub custode, et quidem seruo etc.

[2] This is obvious from the accounts of all the great Othin-heroes, e.g. Sigmundr, Starkaðr, Haraldr Hilditǫnn, Ragnar Loðbrók. Reference may be made also to the conduct of the Eruli, who according to Procopius

the peace and plenty and the semi-priestly government, which, according to Ynglinga s. 12, marked the days of Frö.

It is not quite clear whether Tacitus' information was recent. It might possibly be based on stories heard by the members of Drusus' and Germanicus' expeditions in the early part of the century. On the whole, however, it seems likely that his information was derived through quite a different channel. He passes on to the Suiones, not by way of the Elbe tribes, but by a much more eastern course. The tribes mentioned last before the Suiones are the Gotones, Rugii and Lemouii; after the Suiones he passes immediately to the Aestii. Hence it is not improbable that he derived his information from Nero's agent, who had been sent (apparently by way of Carnuntum) to examine the amber coasts. Tacitus' information will therefore apply to a period shortly after the middle of the first century. Therefore, if any reliance is to be placed on his account, the cult of Othin can not have been known to the Swedes before about A.D. 50.

It has been shown above (1) that the cult of Othin must, in all probability, have been known to the Swedes by about A.D. 500, and (2) that its introduction apparently did not take place before about A.D. 50. For the attainment of a more definite answer there appears to be but one argument available, and this too is one which is usually regarded with the utmost scepticism. Can the introduction of the cult have synchronised with the introduction of the practice of cremation? It has already been mentioned (p. 22) that in Ynglinga s. 8

(Gothic War, II. 14) compelled their king Rudolph to make war against the Langobardi, though they brought forward no excuse except the fact that they had been without war for three years.

the institution of cremation is attributed to Othin:—"He ordained that all dead men should be burnt and brought on to the pyre with their property," etc. I can not see that there is any great inherent improbability in such an assumption. For the practice of burning the dead seems to point towards a view of immortality which was altogether inconsistent with the popular Scandinavian belief. According to this belief the souls of the dead were supposed to live on in the howe in which they were buried. In several cases the ghost is represented as defending his treasure, when the howe is broken open. The howe seems to have been situated close to the family dwelling, and the ancestral spirits were believed to exercise a beneficent influence over the fortunes of the family. Offerings appear to have been paid to them, especially, it would seem, with the view of obtaining fertility for the land. It may be objected that the continuance of the soul's life in the howe would not be affected by the burning of the body. But the souls of those who were burnt according to the ordinances of Othin, were supposed to pass to Valhǫll. The two conceptions are entirely different; for Valhǫll was regarded as far away. In Sǫgubrot af fornkonungum 9 Hringr gives Haraldr a chariot and horse, in order that he may ride or drive to Valhǫll (cf. p. 22 f.). So also in Ynglinga s. 10 Othin, when dying, "said that he was about to journey to Goðheimr and greet his friends there. The Swedes now thought that he had come into the ancient Ásgarðr and would there live for ever." The view expressed in this passage may of course have been influenced to some extent by Christian ideas. Yet, that Valhǫll was regarded as far away, may be inferred from another passage in the same saga (c. 13):—"When all the Swedes knew that Frö

was dead, but plenty and peace continued, they believed
that this would last as long as Frö was in Sweden; so
they would not burn him, but they called him the god
of the world and sacrificed to him ever afterwards for
plenty and peace[1]." In the preceding chapter it is
stated that Frö was laid in a howe. The view of Frö's
immortality here expressed is identical with the belief
in the continued life of the spirits in the family howe.
The reluctance of the Swedes to burn Frö is attributed
to their belief that, if this took place, he would no
longer be with them, but would pass to some other place.
There can scarcely be any doubt, in view of what is stated
of Othin and Niǫrðr, that Valhǫll is the place meant.
But if this belief prevailed in the case of Frö, is there any
adequate reason for doubting the existence of a similar
belief in the case of the family manes? If not, the introduction of cremation can be explained only by supposing
that a revolution had taken place in the Scandinavian
view of immortality.

Icelandic writers were under the erroneous impression
that the practice of burning the body was older than the
practice of howe burial. Thus in the Preface to Heimskringla it is stated:—"The first age is called the age of
burning; all dead men had then to be burnt and 'bauta'-
stones raised to their memory. But after Frö had been
'howe-laid' at Upsala, many princes raised howes no less
than bauta-stones in memory of their kinsmen. But
after Danr the Proud, King of the Danes, had had a howe
made for him, and given orders that after his death he
should be brought there with his royal equipment and

---

[1] þá er allir Svíar vissu at Freyr var dauðr, en hélzt ár ok friðr, þá
trúðu þeir at svá mundi vera, meðan Freyr væri á Svíþióð, ok vildu
eigi brenna hann, ok kǫlluðu hann veraldar goð, blótuðu mest til árs ok
friðar alla ævi síðan.

armour, and his horse with its harness, and much treasure besides, many members of his family did so afterwards; and the age of howe-burial began in Denmark. But the age of burning continued much later among the Swedes and Norwegians[1]." According to Ynglinga saga three of the first nine Swedish kings after Frö were cremated, namely Vanlandi, Dómarr and Agni, besides one, Vísburr, who was burnt alive. The first kings who are stated to have been 'howe-laid' are Alfr and Yngvi, grandsons of Agni; after this howe-burial is frequently mentioned. On the other hand, no king is burnt after Agni except Haki (c. 27), who did not belong to the native dynasty; in his case the cremation took place on a ship. The evidence of Ynglinga saga therefore agrees with the statement in the Preface. Yet the evidence of the monuments has made it clear that howe-burial, in one form or another, was practised from the very earliest times— before the use of any metal was known, whereas cremation first makes its appearance comparatively late in the age of bronze. The statements of the ancient writers however appear to contain a certain amount of truth. Burning, which towards the close of the bronze age, and for some time after the first appearance of iron, appears to have been practically universal, again seems to be partially displaced by howe-burial in the course of the early iron age. The ancient writers were mistaken only in supposing that the practice was new. In reality it was a return to

[1] hin fyrsta ǫld er kǫlluð brunaǫld, þá skyldi brenna alla dauða menn ok reisa eptir bautasteina. en síðan er Freyr hafði heygðr verit at Uppsǫlum, þá gerðu margir hǫfðingiar eigi síðr hauga en bautasteina til minningar eptir frændr sína. en síðan er Danr hinn mikilláti Dana-konungr lét sér haug gera, ok bauð sik þangat bera dauðan með konungs skrúði ok herbúnaði, ok hest hans með sǫðulreiði ok mikit fé annat, en hans ættmenn gerðu margir svá síðan, ok hófst þar haugsǫld þar í Danmǫrk. en lengi síðan hélzt brunaǫld með Svíum ok Norðmǫnnum.

the old native custom. It is possible that the old custom was resumed among the Swedish royal family earlier than elsewhere on account of their traditional relationship to Frö.

I would not, of course, be prepared to go so far as to say that howe-burial was always associated with the cult of Frö and the manes. In the Sǫgubrot of fornkonungum Haraldr Hilditǫnn is howe-laid, though at the same time it is explicitly stated that he is expected to go to Valhǫll[1]. In later times the once intimate association between cremation and the cult of Othin may have been in part forgotten. This may have been due to the combination into one system of the cults of Othin and of Frö. That they were originally quite distinct, and that the latter was the earlier of the two, there can hardly be any serious doubt. It is likely that a reminiscence of the struggle between the two cults is preserved in the story of the war between the Aesir and the Vanir (cf. Golther, Mythologie, p. 222 f.).

The data available for ascertaining the period at which cremation began to be practised in the North, are very scanty. It is agreed that cremation was known before the introduction of iron. According to Montelius (Civilisation of Sweden, p. 46; cf. Nordisk Tidskrift, 1884, p. 25) the age of bronze in the North lasted from about B.C. 1500 to about B.C. 500, iron first coming into use about the latter date. Since cremation belongs roughly to the latter half of this period, its introduction, according to Montelius' calculation, will have taken place about B.C. 1000. If this calculation is correct, the introduction of the practice of cremation can not have been due to the cult of Othin; for the latter seems not to have been known to the

---

[1] According to Saxo's account he was cremated (cf. p. 22).

Swedes at the beginning of the present era. But there seems to be considerable doubt as to whether Montelius' conclusions are correct. Worsaae's calculations (Prehistory of the North, p. 75) differ from those of Montelius by at least 500 years. He holds (Prehistory, p. 113) that there is scarcely sufficient evidence for the existence of an iron-culture in full force even in Denmark during the first century of the present era. In reality the first antiquities, to which an approximate date can be assigned with any degree of probability, are the articles found in the bogs of Thorsbjærg and Nydam. These deposits are attributed by Montelius (Nordisk Tidskrift, 1884, p. 25) to the third century, by Wimmer (Runenschrift², p. 302 f.) to the beginning of the fifth century. We shall probably not go very far wrong in concluding that they belong to about the fourth century. These deposits prove the existence at this time of a fully developed iron culture in South Jutland. At Thorsbjærg many sword-hilts and spear-shafts were found, though the iron was all decomposed. The Nydam deposit contained over a hundred swords and from five to six hundred spear-heads. The shafts of the spears varied from eight to ten feet in length (cf. Engel-hardt, Denmark in the Early Iron Age, pp. 52 f., 57). Iron had therefore completely displaced bronze as a material for weapons. But this can not prove that iron was known more than two hundred years earlier. For the transition from the exclusive use of bronze to a fully developed iron equipment two centuries is an ample allowance. In South Jutland therefore the age of bronze may have lasted till the beginning of the second century. There is nothing improbable in such an assumption. Among the Germans with whom Tacitus was acquainted, presumably those living between the Rhine and the Elbe, in the latter part of the first century, the iron-culture was by no means so

far developed as among the South Jutlanders in the fourth
century. He says distinctly (Germ. 6) that iron was not
plentiful; consequently few of them possessed swords or
long spears; the usual weapon was a javelin with a short
and thin iron head. Beyond the Eider the equipment
may well have been still more primitive. It is not unlikely that the "short swords" (breues gladii) used by the
eastern tribes (Gotones, Rugii, Lemouii; Germ. 43) were
made of bronze. But if bronze was still used by the
inhabitants of the southern and south-western coasts of
the Baltic up to the end of the first or the beginning of
the second century, it is likely enough that another century
may have elapsed before iron came into anything like
general use in Sweden. I can not see that there is any
improbability in supposing that the iron age proper did
not begin in Sweden before the third century. It has
been mentioned above that the western Germans of
Tacitus' time were still in what may be called a rudimentary iron age. But among the Slavs in the sixth
century the iron-culture appears to have been no further
developed than among Tacitus' Germans. Like the latter
they carried no arms except a shield and javelin (Procopius,
Gothic War, III. 14). This illustrates the slowness with
which the knowledge of the metals travelled. The original
home of the Slavs lay no further from the boundaries of
Roman civilisation than did that of the Swedes, though
in the case of the Slavs there was of course a racial barrier
to be overcome. Taking all considerations together, it
seems to me probable that the degree of progress in the
knowledge of the metals, which we find among the western
Germans in the first century, and among the Slavs in the
sixth century, is scarcely likely to have been reached by
the Swedes before the third or fourth century. Isolated
iron weapons may of course have penetrated occasionally

to the North before this time[1]. Yet this is not enough
to constitute even a rudimentary iron age in the true
sense.

Between the adoption of the practice of cremation and
the beginning of the rudimentary iron-culture some considerable time must have elapsed; but the calculation of
centuries in such a case can be nothing more than mere
guess-work. If the rudimentary iron-culture began in the
third century, it is by no means impossible that the
adoption of cremation took place in the first century.
Hence if cremation is to be associated in any way with
the cult of Othin, it is during the latter part of the
first century that we must suppose the cult to have been
introduced into Sweden. This hypothesis receives some
slight support from a statement in Tacitus (Germ. 40).
He says that seven northern tribes worshipped the goddess
Nerthus, i.e. Mother Earth, "on an island in the ocean."
There can be no serious doubt that this goddess Nerthus
is closely related to the Scandinavian god Niǫrðr. A rite
very similar to that described by Tacitus was practised by
the Swedes in connection with the worship of Frö (Freyr)
the son of Niǫrðr. The festival of Nerthus was accompanied by a holy peace; wars were not undertaken, and
weapons were put away; "peace and quiet are then only
known and loved" until the goddess returns to her temple.
From this description it seems likely enough that the cult
of Woden-Othin prevailed among these tribes, but that it
was combined to some extent with the older cult of
Nerthus-Niǫrðr. Since Niǫrðr and Frö were essentially
gods of peace, it is probable that the holy peace which
was kept at certain seasons (perhaps the new year), was a

[1] It is likely that for a long time afterwards swords and other weapons
were largely of foreign manufacture. Several of the swords found in the
bogs of South Jutland bear Roman marks.

survival from this earlier cult. Now it has been rashly assumed by many writers that the island on which the temple stood was necessarily situated in the North Sea. But there is absolutely no evidence for this assumption; in cc. 43, 44 "*oceanus*" is clearly used of parts of the Baltic. There is no island in the North Sea large enough to fulfil the conditions required in Germ. 40. Hence Much (P. B. B. XVII. 196 ff.) and Sarazzin (Anglia, XIX. 384) have conjectured with great probability that the island mentioned by Tacitus is in reality the island of Seeland. If this is really the case, and if in Tacitus' time the cult of Woden-Othin had already made its way so far north, there is nothing strange in supposing that it may have become known to the Swedes in the course of the next generation.

The conclusions attained in the course of this discussion may be briefly summarised as follows:—(1) The cult of Othin was in all probability known in the North at the beginning of the sixth century; there is no reason for supposing that it was then new. (2) The cult does not seem to have been practised by the Swedes in the first half-century of the present era. (3) If the adoption of cremation was due to the cult of Othin, the cult can hardly have been introduced into Sweden later than the end of the first century.

NOTE I.

The Name of the God.

The original meaning of the words *Wōðanaz (O. Sax. Wōdan, O.H.G. wuotan) and *Wōðenaz (O.E. Wōden, O.N. Oðinn) is much disputed. Some take the word to be related to Sk. vāta- 'wind,' and consequently regard Woden as having been originally a god of wind and storm. This etymology is improbable as Golther (Mythologie, p. 293, footnote) has shown; vāta- represents in all probability an Idg. *u̯ēto- and is closely related to Lat. uentus. Golther (Mythologie, p. 292 ff.) holds that Woden is a deified development of Wode, the leader of the ghostly army (das wütende Heer) which is supposed to dash through the air on stormy nights. Kluge (Wb.⁵ p. 412 b; cf. Bradke, Dyâus Asura, p. x, footnote) while admitting a relationship between Woden and das wütende Heer, connects the former with Lat. uātes, O. Ir. fáith, and hence concludes that the god had originally a bardic character. Golther's hypothesis is especially favoured by Adam of Bremen's expression 'Wodan, id est furor' (IV. 26; cf. O.E. wodendream = furor animi, Gloss.), and by the fact that in Sweden 'das wütende Heer' is known as 'Odens jagt.' Yet one must surely reckon with the possibility that this superstition may have received its name from later association with the Woden-mythology. Golther also overstates the case against the connection of Wōden with Lat. uātes etc., when he protests that this assumes for the cult in its initial stages, a character which it can have attained only in its latest and highest development. When the cult first makes its appearance, namely in the first century, Woden is rendered by *Mercurius*, an identification which would be inexplicable, unless the higher side of the god's character was already to some extent developed. Golther's objection is based on the assumption that the cult was native among the Germans. If on the other hand the cult was introduced from abroad, the god may very well have been associated from the beginning with all those attributes by which he was characterised in later times.

If the word *wōden* is related to *uātes*, it does not necessarily follow that the god had originally a bardic character. Among the Gauls the 'uates' were distinct from the 'bardi,' cf. Strabo, IV. 4, 4 :—"The bards are minstrels and poets, but the uates are offerers of sacrifices and interpreters of nature[1]." Diodorus (V. 31) renders *uates* by μάντεις. It can scarcely be denied that the 'uates,' who seems to have combined the offices of soothsayer and sacrificial priest, bears a certain resemblance to Othin (Woden); for the latter is distinguished above all else by his skill in sorcery. It is perhaps worth mention that Othin appears as *Uggerus* (i.e. Yggr) *uates* in Saxo, V. p. 238.

On the whole therefore Kluge's explanation seems to me the most probable. The word *wōðanaz—*wōðenaz* seems to be participial in form and may originally have denoted 'inspired.' It is likely enough that the word is related both to O.E. *wōd* (=*rabidus uel insanus*, Gloss.) and to O.E. *wōþ* (=*facundia*, Gloss.)[2].

---

[1] βάρδοι μὲν ὑμνηταὶ καὶ ποιηταί, οὐάτεις δὲ ἱεροποιοὶ καὶ φυσιολόγοι.

[2] cf. Kluge, l.c.; Kaufmann, Mythologie, p. 42 f.

NOTE II.

The following story is told in Gautreks s. 7 (F. A. S. III.
32 f.), immediately after the account of the lot-casting, through
which king Vikar lost his life (cf. p. 3). Shortly before
midnight Starkaðr was awakened by his foster-father Hrosshársgrani, and told to follow him. They took a small boat
and rowed out to an island. Then they went up into the
forest and came to a clearing, in which an assembly of
considerable size was being held. Eleven men were seated on
chairs, and there was another chair vacant. They came into
the assembly and Hrosshársgrani sat down on the vacant
chair. He was greeted by all as Othin. He said that they
were assembled in order to decide Starkaðr's fate. Then Thor
began as follows :—"Alfhildr, the mother of Starkaðr's father,
chose a cunning giant, in preference to Ásaþórr, to be the
father of her son. I decree that Starkaðr shall have neither
son nor daughter. His line shall thus come to an end."
Othin answered :—"I decree that he shall live for three
generations." Thor said :—"He shall work a dastardly deed
in each generation." Othin : "I decree that he shall have
the best of weapons and clothes." Thor : "I decree that he
shall have neither land nor fief." Othin : "I grant him that
he shall have moveable property in abundance." Thor : "I
determine that he shall never think he has enough." Othin :
"I give him victory and prowess in every battle." Thor : "I
determine that he shall receive a severe wound in every

battle." Othin: "I grant him the gift of poetry, so that he shall be able to compose as fast as he can speak." Thor: "He shall not be able to remember what he composes." Othin: "I decree that he shall receive the greatest favour from the noblest and best of men." Thor: "He shall be detested by all the commons." They passed all these decrees about Starkaðr's fate, and the assembly then broke up. Hrosshársgrani then asks Starkaðr to reward him for the favourable decrees which he had made for him, and when Starkaðr signifies assent he demands his assistance in procuring Vikar's death: "thou shalt send king Vikar to me" (cf. p. 3 f.).

This story is instructive in two respects. It shows, firstly, that Othin was thought to preside over certain departments of human life, while others were controlled by Thor. Othin grants (1) prolongation of life. According to Saxo[1] VI. p. 276 Othinus granted to Starcatherus thrice the ordinary span of life, in return for the sacrifice of Vicarus. With this may be compared the sacrifice of Aun (Ynglinga s. 29), who obtains prolongation of life by sacrificing one of his sons to Othin every tenth year. Othin grants (2) choice weapons and clothes and abundance of moveable wealth. With this may be compared Hyndlulióð 2:—"He (Othin) makes grants and presents of gold to his following; he gave Hermóðr a helmet and coat of mail, and presented Sigmundr with a sword" (cf. p. 51)[2]. Othin is (3) the giver of victory. This requires no illustration (cf. p. 5 f.). He is (4) the giver of poetry (skáldskapr); cf. Saxo VI. p. 276:—"He endowed Starcatherus not only with valour but also with skill in the composition of

---

[1] The story related above does not occur in Saxo.

[2] hann geldr ok gefr
gull verðungu:
gaf hann Hermóði
hiálm ok bryniu,
ok Sigmundi
sverð at þiggia.

songs[1]." So according to Ynglinga s. 6 : "He (Othin) made
all his speeches in verse in the same way in which we now
recite what is called *skáldskapr*. He and his temple-priests
are called song-smiths (*lióðasmiðir*) because they originated
this art in the North." Hyndlulióð 3 may also be compared : " He gives victory to some and money to others;
eloquence and wisdom he grants to many men. He gives fair
breezes to captains and diction to poets; valour he grants to
many a champion[2]." Lastly Othin promises Starkaðr the
favour of the nobility, while Thor denies him the good will of
the commons. This agrees with the fact that the cult of
Othin seems to have been practised chiefly, if not exclusively,
at the courts of kings and nobles, while Thor remained the
god of the commons. Hárbarðslióð 24 may be compared :—
" Othin possesses the nobles who fall in battle, but Thor has
the race of serfs[3]." On the other hand not only the good will
of the commons, but also the granting of land and of children
seem to be out of Othin's power. In the latter case Frö was
perhaps more frequently invoked than Thor[4]; but probably
the granting of land was usually attributed to Thor. He is
called *landáss* "god of the land," and seems to have been the
patron of the assembly. But these distinctions between the
powers of the various gods may in part hold good only for the
later days of heathendom, and were even then not always
strictly observed. The story is important chiefly for its

[1] Starcatherum......non solum animi fortitudine, sed eciam condendo-
rum carminum pericia illustrauit.

[2] gefr hann sigr sumum,
en sumum aura,
mælsku mǫrgum
ok mannvit firum
byri gefr hann brǫgnum
en brag skaldum,
gefr hann mannsemi
mǫrgum rekki.

[3] Cf. p. 26 f. and the passage from Saxo there quoted.
[4] Cf. Adam of Bremen iv. 26.

account of the blessings which the worshipper of Othin was supposed to enjoy.

Secondly, the story shows that the relations between Thor and Starkaðr were essentially different from those between Othin and Starkaðr. Othin's decrees are all blessings; Thor's are the reverse. Thor is only once mentioned by Saxo in the passages which deal with Starcatherus, namely VI. p. 274, where it is stated that Starcatherus was supposed to have been of giant origin and had originally many hands, all of which except two were stripped off by Thor. But since Thor is always represented as hostile to giants, it may reasonably be inferred that he was hostile also to Starcatherus. Again it is perhaps worth mention that according to Saxo, VI. p. 278 Starcatherus, after staying seven years in Sweden with the sons of Frö, was so disgusted with the rites practised at the Upsala sacrifices, that he returned to Denmark. This passage seems to show that Starkaðr was hostile to the worship of Frö. On the other hand he is very closely associated with the cult of Othin; for according to Gautreks saga Othin was his foster-father. The story of his compact with Othin and the consequent sacrifice of Vikar is known both to Gautreks saga and to Saxo.

Starkaðr has usually been regarded as the typical Northern warrior of old time. This is true; but in reality he is far more. He is also the chief of the legendary Northern poets. If I am not mistaken, he was regarded in early times as the typical worshipper of Othin.

NOTE III.

THE INTERPRETATION OF HÁVAMÁL 138 f.

It has been customary in recent years to trace various features in the Othin-mythology to Christian sources. Some of the theories put forward on this subject appear at first sight more or less plausible. Practically however the whole question rests on the interpretation of Hávamál 138 f. If the explanation of this passage adopted by Munch and Bugge be accepted, many of the other theories may deserve consideration; if on the other hand this explanation be rejected, few will probably attach much importance to the rest. The passage runs as follows :—138 "I know that I hung full nine nights on the gallows tree (or "windy tree") wounded by the javelin and given to Othin, myself to myself; on that tree, of which no one knows from whose roots it proceeds." 139. "They cheered me (or "assuaged my hunger and thirst") neither with bread nor drink; I looked down and took up runes, took them up crying; from thence I fell again[1]."

[1] veit ek at ek hekk
vindga meiði á,
nætr allar níu,
geiri undaðr
ok gefinn Óðni,
siálfr siálfum mér ;
á þeim meiði
er mangi veit
hvers hann af rótum renn.

við hleifi mik seldu
né við hornigi,

According to Bugge's theory the Norse vikings became acquainted with Christian doctrines in their expeditions among the Western Islands during the ninth century. These doctrines, though at first totally foreign to the ideas of the Northern religion, yet became in course of time assimilated and transferred to Othin. I am not prepared altogether to deny the possibility of such a transference of religious ideas. Whether such particulars as the story of Leucius and Carinus (Bugge, Studier, p. 334 ff.) could be thus orally acquired seems to me more doubtful. Yet it is not absolutely impossible that some Northern bard should have had access to written texts. These details however are scarcely material to the main point.

According to Golther (Mythologie, p. 350), who in the main follows Bugge, there are two decisive points which establish the Christian origin of the story recounted in Háv. 138 f. These are (1) that the god sacrificed himself; (2) that the gallows-tree, which was used for this purpose, became thereby emblematic of the world. These two points require separate treatment. It will be convenient to begin with the latter.

The identity of the world-tree with the tree on which Othin hung is inferred from the following facts : 1. The world-tree is called *Yggdrasill* (or *Askr Yggdrasils*), which is supposed to mean "Othin's horse"; 2. There is an unmistakeable correspondence between the closing words of Háv. 138 :

> á þeim meiði,
> er mangi veit,
> hvers hann af rótum renn.

> > nýsta ek niðr,
> > nam ek upp rúnar,
> > oepandi nam,
> > fell ek aptr þaðan.

On the interpretation of vindga meiði (138, 2) and seldu (139, 1) see Bugge, Studier, pp. 292 f., 345 n. 3; Magnússon, Odin's Horse, pp. 18 footnote and 27 ff.

"on that tree of which no one knows, from whose roots it proceeds," and Fiǫlsvinnsmál 19, 20 :

> hvat þat barr heitir,
> er breiðask um
> lǫnd ǫll limar?

> Míma-meiðr hann heitir,
> enn þat mangi veit,
> af hverium rótum renn.

"What is that tree[1] called, whose branches spread over all lands?" 20. "It is called 'Mima'—tree, but no one knows from what roots it proceeds."

The hypothesis that *Yggdrasill* means 'Othin's horse,' in the sense of 'the horse (i.e. gallows) ridden by Othin,' does not seem to me to be satisfactorily established. In the first place the use of a compound instead of a dependent genitive in such a case is at least curious. *Yggr* is indeed a frequent name of Othin, but originally it would seem to have been merely an epithet. Though the word never occurs except as a name of Othin, is it not possible that in the compound its original sense may have been preserved—perhaps 'horse of terror' or something of the kind? Secondly, even if it be granted that *Yggdrasill* must mean 'Othin's horse' in the sense of 'gallows,' it does not necessarily follow that it denotes the gallows on which Othin himself hung. It might equally well denote the gallows on which Othin's victims were hanged.

Again, though there can scarcely be any doubt that some relationship exists between Háv. 138, 7—9 and Fiǫlsv. 20, the nature of this relationship is not so clear. It is unlikely that the somewhat awkward *hvers hann af rótum renn* of Hávamál should be taken from the simpler *af hverium rótum renn* of Fiǫlsvinnsmál. It is possible, however, that Háv. 138

---

[1] *barr* in reality denotes 'spine of a fir' etc. If the text is right, the poet can not have known the meaning of the word.

is not the original passage in which these words occurred. The strophe is too long by three lines for the lióðaháttr metre, and it is hardly unreasonable to suggest that these three lines may be a later addition from some other (lost) poem. The motive for the interpolation would be the desire to explain *vindga meiði* in l. 2[1].

It is at least remarkable that, in all the passages which deal with the world-tree, there is not a single reference to its having served as Othin's gallows. Yet, according to Golther (pp. 350, 529 f.), it was precisely through this that the idea of a world-tree arose. Bugge also, while allowing that the people of the North may in very early times have conceived of a great, marvellous and holy tree, which did not belong to this earth, yet goes on to state (p. 527) that the subsequent development of this idea was due to Christian influences, and that the holy tree only obtained its full significance as 'world-tree' from its association with the Cross.

By far the most important parallel to the world-tree seems to me to be furnished by the description of the Upsala tree in Schol. 134 to Adam of Bremen: *prope templum est arbor maxima late ramos extendens, aestate et hyeme semper uirens: cuius illa generis sit nemo scit.* There is not an expression in this account which does not apply in some measure also to the world-tree. With *late ramos extendens* may be compared Fiǫlsv. 19: *es breiðask um lǫnd ǫll limar;* with *aestate et hyeme semper uirens* may be compared Vǫl. R. 18: *stendr æ yfir groenn Urðar brunni,* 'it (i.e. the ash) stands ever green over the well of Urðr (Fate).' Again, though Bugge expresses some doubt on the point, there is at least a striking similarity between the expression *cuius illa generis sit nemo scit* and Fiǫlsv. 20: *en þat mangi veit af hverium rótum renn.* Possibly the scholiast here may have misunderstood his information. Again, the first words of

---

[1] Magnússon (Odin's Horse, p. 22) retains ll. 7—9 and regards ll. 4—6 as interpolated (*geiri undaðr | ok gefinn Óðni, | sialfr sialfum mér*). But I do not see what could have given rise to such a curious interpolation.

the scholion: *prope templum est arbor maxima* etc. may be
compared with Grimnismál 25 :

> Heiðrún heitir geit,
> er stendr hǫllo á Heriafǫðrs
> ok bítr af Læraðs limom etc.

"There is a goat called Heiðrun which stands on Heriafǫðr's
(Othin's) hall and bites from the branches of Læraðr"—and
26 :

> Eikþyrnir heitir hiǫrtr,
> er stendr á hǫllo Heriafǫðrs,
> ok bítr af Læraðs limom etc.

"There is a hart called Eikþyrnir" etc. It is clear from
these passages that the tree Læraðr stood close to the hall
(Valhǫll). According to the usual view, which is accepted
by Bugge (p. 483 ; cf. also Golther, p. 529), Læraðr is either
identical with Yggdrasill, or denotes the upper branches of
the same. The description of the tree (or grove) Glasir in
Skaldskaparmál 36 may also be compared :

> Glasir stendr
> með gullnu laufi
> firir Sigtýs sǫlum.

"Glasir stands with golden foliage in front of Sigtýr's
(Othin's) halls." It is uncertain whether Glasir is identical
with Yggdrasill or not. Again, with the expression *arbor
maxima* may be compared Vǫl. R. 18 : *hár baðmr heilagr*.
Lastly, in the same scholion, immediately after the description of the tree, occurs the following sentence : *ibi etiam est
fons ubi sacrificia paganorum solent exerceri et homo uiuus
immergi*, etc. Though the relative positions of the tree and
the spring are not indicated, it might reasonably be inferred
from the passage that they were not far apart. Here, therefore, again may be compared the words of Vǫl. R. 18 :
(Yggdrasill) *stendr æ yfir groenn Urðar brunni*.

Bugge (p. 502) seems to me to have greatly underrated

the importance of this scholion in its bearing upon the world-tree. He says there is no definite reference to the idea of a world-tree in the scholion, though (following Nyerup) he admits that the Upsala tree might possibly be a copy of the world-tree. On the other hand Mannhardt (Baumkultus, p. 57, foot-note) adduces a parallel from the account of Bishop Otto's journey to Stettin, A.D. 1124 (M. G. XII. 794): *erat praeterea ibi quercus ingens et frondosa, et fons subter eam amoenissimus, quam plebs simplex numinis alicuius inhabitatione sacram existimans magna ueneratione colebat.* When the bishop wished to destroy the oak, the inhabitants succeeded in dissuading him saying: *saluare illam potius quam saluari ab illa se uelle.* This passage shows that similar tree-sanctuaries were known on the continent[1]. It is impossible therefore to withstand Mannhardt's conclusion that 'Nyerup's Hypothese ist umzukehren.' This conclusion is further supported by the fact that the property assigned to the world-tree (Mimameiðr) in Fiǫlsv. 22 :

> út af hans aldni
> skal á eld bera
> fyr killisiúkar konur.

"Some of its fruit is to be taken out and burnt for the sake of women who are in travail[2]" is identical with that popularly assigned to the 'Vårdträd' (cf. Mannhardt, p. 56). So also the position occupied by the Vårdträd in close proximity to the family house corresponds not only to that of the Upsala tree beside the temple, but also to that of

---

[1] They seem to have been especially important among the Lithuanians and Prussians, cf. Aeneas Sylvius, Hist. de Europa, XXVI.; S. Grunau, Preussische Chronik, Tract. 2, Cap. V. § 2; Tract. 3, Cap. I. § 2. It is noteworthy that the sacred oak of the Prussians, like the tree at Upsala, was *stets grün, winter und sommer*.

[2] Killisiúkar is an emendation suggested by Bugge. The MSS. have kelisiúkar ('hysterical,' according to Vigfusson). It is perhaps worth notice that among the ancient Prussians, according to Lucas David I. 137 f. (quoted by Voigt, Geschichte Preussens I. 583), the embers of the sacred fire of oak-wood were credited with medicinal properties.

Lærað (and Glasir) beside Valhǫll. Even Bugge (p. 499) admits that these holy ashes have influenced the doctrine of Yggdrasill. But I fail to see what elements in the conception of Yggdrasill could not have been developed out of the Vårdträd. Just as Valhǫll, the warrior-paradise, is a copy of an earthly court, so Yggdrasill may be copied from the Vårdträd which stood beside the court. Yggdrasill is by no means consistently represented as including all things; besides the passage quoted above (p. 76) from Skáldskaparmál, mention may also be made of Grimn. 29, which represents the gods as coming to exercise justice under the ash Yggdrasill—a picture which may very well be drawn from real life. There are indeed only two poetic passages in which the ash Yggdrasill is definitely represented as a 'world-tree,' namely Fiǫlsv. 19 (cf. p. 74) and Grimn. 31. In the latter case it is stated that Hel, the Hrímþursar and the human race dwell under the three roots of the tree. In all other passages Yggdrasill may be interpreted as a heavenly Vårdträd. It is true that much is obscure in the representation of Yggdrasill, e.g. the use of the words *miǫtviðr* in Vǫl. R. 2 and *miǫtuðr* in Fiǫlsv. 20 (and Vǫl. R. 46 ?). Yet I can see no great difficulty involved in the transition from the conception of Yggdrasill as a tree whose life is bound up with the fate of the world to its conception as an all-comprehending world-tree. The association of Yggdrasill with the fate of the world comes naturally enough from its character as the Vårdträd of the gods. The different stages in the growth of the conception may briefly be indicated as follows : (1) Each community has a (material) Vårdträd, the life of which is bound up with the fate of the community ; the tree at Upsala would seem to have been the Vårdträd of the Swedish nation (though originally it was no doubt the Vårdträd of the local community). (2) When Valhǫll became depicted after the likeness of a human community, it had necessarily to be provided with a Vårdträd of its own. (3) When the conceptions of Valhǫll and Ásgarð became confused and a complex theological system resulted; and when at the same time speculation began to pass beyond the ideas of family and tribe, and to take the whole human race into account, there arose the idea of 'the world,' a community embracing all beings, human, divine and demonic. This community was then provided with its Vårdträd, Yggdrasill, the life of which was bound up with the fate of the world.

The properties of the heavenly immaterial Yggdrasill seem to have been transferred thereto from its earthly material prototype. This applies not merely to its size, its position and its medicinal properties, but also to the uncertainty felt as to its origin, at least if the words *cuius illa generis sit nemo scit* have anything to do with *mangi veit af hverium rótum renn*. These words need not denote the immaterial character of the tree, but rather may mean simply that the seed from which it sprang was unknown. Therefore, though in Fiǫlsvinnsmál the expression *af hverium rótum renn* is applied to the heavenly Yggdrasill, this need not be the case with the parallel *hvers hann af rótum renn* in Hávamál. These words may be nothing more than a poetical circumlocution for Vårdträd. So also with regard to the name *Yggdrasill*, it has been shown (p. 74) that, even if this means 'Othin's horse,' it does not necessarily imply that it was the horse (i.e. gallows) which Othin himself rode; it might also denote the gallows on which Othin's victims were made to ride. There is indeed no explicit statement to the effect that Othin's victims were hanged on the Vårdträd, but there is nothing improbable in the idea. Adam of Bremen (IV. 27) states in his account of the Upsala sacrifice: *corpora* (i.e. of the victims) *autem suspenduntur in lucum qui proximus est templo. is enim lucus tam sacer est gentilibus ut singulae arbores eius ex morte uel tabo immolatorum diuinae credantur.* What relation the 'tree' in Schol. 134 bears to the 'grove' in the text is not clear, but there is nothing improbable in supposing that it formed part thereof. Hence I can not see that there is any valid reason for disbelieving that the name

Yggdrasill may have been applied to the earthly Vårdträd,
and transferred together with the conception of the tree to its
heavenly copy.   It is perhaps worth calling to mind that the
name *Sleipnir* is used for a gallows in Ynglingatál (Yngl.
s. 28).

It is assumed both by Bugge (p. 297 ff.) and Golther
(p. 350) that the sacrifice was a self-sacrifice on the part
of Othin.   Yet this is not stated in the text.   The words
gefinn Óðni sialfr sialfum mêr can, so far as I can see, mean
nothing more than 'given to Othin myself to myself," i.e.
Othin is both the person sacrificed and the person to whom
the sacrifice is offered.   There is no indication that Othin was
also the sacrificer or that the sacrifice was voluntary on the
part of the victim.   The words of the Shetland song quoted
by Bugge (p. 309), whatever may be its value, practically
exclude such an interpretation; and they derive a certain
amount of support from the opening lines of Háv: 139.   The
statement of Bugge and Golther, so far as it has any foundation at all, must be an inference from Ynglinga s. 10, where
the dying Othin is represented as having himself marked with
the point of a javelin (*lét hann marka sik geirsoddi;* cf. p. 13 f.).
It is of course by no means certain that the events related in
the two passages (Háv. 138 and Yngl. 10) are the same.   If
their identity be not admitted, Bugge's (and Golther's) assumption must be rejected as baseless.   The identification
is however ingenious, and on the whole I am rather inclined
to think it may be right.   The chief difficulty is that there is
no reference to hanging in Ynglinga s. 10.   But in the
following chapter Niǫrðr also is represented as having himself
marked with a javelin before his death (cf. p. 14).   Niǫrðr
is identical with Saxo's Hadingus who commits suicide by
hanging himself (i. p. 60; see above, pp. 17, 35).

The acceptance of this identification does not of course
involve the adoption of Bugge's theory.   A far more probable

explanation of the myth is that it arose out of the desire
to explain the ritual of sacrifice. Othin is above all a god of
the dead, and his abode is the 'hall of the slain'; but how
far the ancients in heathen times conceived of his having
lived upon the earth, is not clear. So soon as this belief had
arisen, and with it the idea that he passed to Valhǫll by
death, the conditions for the conception of the gallows-myth
were at hand. Possibly also a misunderstanding of the
term 'Othin's horse' (*Yggdrasill, Sleipnir*), as a name of the
gallows-tree, may have contributed to this end. The objection
urged by Golther (p. 350; cf. also Bugge, p. 304) against the
view here put forward, namely that Othin would not be
represented as choosing the form of death which was suffered
by prisoners of war, is unfounded. This method of death was
sacrificial, and though in later times the victims were no
doubt usually prisoners, slaves or criminals, this appears
not to have been the case in the earlier stages of the religion
(cf. p. 27 f.). It is sufficient here to refer to the case of
Hadingus—Niǫrðr.

The bearing of the story related in Gautreks s. 7 (p. 3 f.)
on Háv. 138 is obvious. The nature of the connection
between the two passages ought to be equally clear, namely
that we have in both cases a picture of the ordinary ritual
of sacrifice to Othin. I can not see the slightest ground for
supposing with Bugge (p. 315) that the story in Gautreks
saga has been influenced by the myth of Othin's hanging.
That it should be based on the passage in Hávamál is incredible.

Lastly some reference must be made to the interpretation
of Háv. 141. According to Bugge and Golther the idea of
Othin's increased vitality in this verse is consequent on his
death in str. 139. Golther (p. 349) goes so far as to regard
str. 140 as an interpolation, and Bugge (p. 353, n. 3) seems
inclined to think it has got out of its right place. But I can
see no obvious reason why str. 140 should have been inserted
here, if this was not its original place. Again, I can not see

why str. 141 should have any reference to str. 139. The
natural interpretation is to take str. 138, 139 together as
an episode complete in itself, and str. 140, 141 as another
episode, Othin's increased vitality being represented as due to
his acquisition of Óðrerir. The key-words to the whole
passage seem to me to be the almost synonymous *rún* and
lióð. These serve to connect the two episodes, and at the
same time to link them on both to what goes before
(str. 137 and the preceding strophes) and to what follows.
There seems to me to be no need for any change in the order
of the strophes.

For EU product safety concerns, contact us at Calle de José Abascal, 56–1°, 28003 Madrid, Spain or eugpsr@cambridge.org.

 www.ingramcontent.com/pod-product-compliance
Ingram Content Group UK Ltd.
Pitfield, Milton Keynes, MK11 3LW, UK
UKHW012334130625
459647UK00009B/269